Praise for Rev. Dr. Susan Thistlethwai...
controversial and must-read n...

D0006072

Susan Brooks Thistlethwaite brings ... scholar, the spirit of a pastor and the ... #OccupytheBible. *Her book reveals th... relevancy of the sacred scriptures for today's struggling world and offers a compelling altar call for Christians to live out the mandate for justice inherent within our faith.*

—The Reverend Paul Raushenbush, Religion Editor,
The Huffington Post

The power and clarity of Dr. Thistlethwaite's book confronts an anemic church afraid of the words and witness of Jesus Christ. This is a must-read for all who want to reclaim the Bible and the Church from poor biblical scholarship and a market-driven theology possessed by Wall Street. Read at your own risk. You may accept the call to #occupytheworld with love and justice.

—The Reverend Otis Moss, III, Senior Pastor,
Trinity United Church of Christ, Chicago, IL

This book is a must-read for Christians struggling to follow Jesus in an era of rampant greed as well as those concerned that America's economic system is morally bankrupt. The book's grounding in scripture and theology is a critical tool for anyone trying to counter hypocritical political leaders or Christian right leaders who are leading America astray on economic policies and principles.

—The Reverend Jennifer Butler, Executive Director,
Faith in Public Life

Many serious-minded faith leaders still cannot articulate why the Occupy movement engaged them so powerfully or why its distinctive culture continues to fascinate. For all such leaders this book will come as a huge gift. Susan Thistlethwaite uses compelling scholarship to show just how biblically and theologically relevant the Occupy movement was and is. It doesn't matter that the encampments are gone; this book is about us: it is about our calling and our need to do a "mic check" on a money-dominated social system that is rapidly losing its way.

—The Reverend Peter Laarman, Executive Director,
Progressive Christians Uniting

Susan Brooks Thistlethwaite inspires, educates, and challenges me [us] to deeper biblical understanding about what God intends for us to do as His people at this time in America's economic travails. She is a prophet who in my evangelical theological tradition engages not in predictions or foretelling as much as forth telling, applying truth to contemporary circumstances. It is clear, insightful, and oh so relevant. I wish every evangelical in America would read this book. It will change you, one way or another.

—The Reverend Richard Cizik, President, The New
Evangelical Partnership for the Common Good

With signs of religious decline all around, many wonder if the church has a future. In this provocative book, Susan Brooks Thistlethwaite points to another sign for the church—a hopeful one: the Occupy movement. As she explores Occupy in light of scripture, it becomes clear that the church must renew itself as a grassroots movement of those who enact Jesus' teaching to love God and neighbor. Is Occupy a sign of a new spiritual awakening? Thistlethwaite thinks so, and I suspect she is right.

—Diana Butler Bass, Ph.D., author,
Christianity After Religion: The End of Church and the Birth of a New Spiritual Awakening

Susan Thistlethwaite's new book, #OccupytheBible, *is a powerful reminder for LGBT people of faith everywhere that economic justice is, at heart, a queer issue. Jesus of Nazareth had a preferential option for the poor and the marginalized—that is, the queer folk of his day. Read this amazing book and take back the Bible by unleashing your own biblical Stonewall Rebellion!*

—The Rev. Patrick S. Cheng, Ph.D., Associate
Professor of Historical and Systematic Theology,
Episcopal Divinity School

#OccupytheBible

What Jesus Really Said (and Did) About Money and Power

By

Rev. Dr. Susan Brooks Thistlethwaite

ASTOR + BLUE EDITIONS

#OCCUPYTHEBIBLE: WHAT JESUS REALLY SAID (AND DID) ABOUT MONEY AND POWER

Astor + Blue Editions

Copyright © 2012 Rev. Dr. Susan B. Thistlethwaite

All rights reserved. Except for brief passages quoted in newspapers, magazines, radio, television, websites, and blogs, no part of this book may be reproduced in any form or by any means, electronic or mechanical, including photocopying and recording, or by any information storage and retrieval system, without written permission from the Publisher.

Astor + Blue Editions
New York, NY 10003
www.astorandblue.com

1. Excerpts from the following works are published by permission of Astor + Blue Editions: Biblical quotations, unless otherwise indicated in the text, are from:

New Revised Standard Version Bible, copyright 1989, Division of Christian Education of the National Council of the Churches of Christ in the United States of America. Used by permission. All rights reserved.

All columns previously published on the *Washington Post On Faith* page online are used according to the editorial guidelines of the On Faith page.

2. All Photographs are printed with permission by Astor + Blue Editions. Arturas Rosenbacher, page 2; John C. Goodwin, page 13; Mario Tama/Getty Images News, page 16; Corbis/Bettman Collection, page 34; REUTERS/Brian Nguyen, page 36; Ilias Bartolini, page 41; Brown Brothers, page 58; The Everett Collection, page 58; Corbis, page 63; Walter P. Reuther Library, page 83; The Star-Ledger, page 85; Associated Press/Jacquelyn Martin, page 99; Mary Ann Sullivan, page 115; Timothy Krause, page 120; Nubar Alexanian, page 130; Paul Weiskel, page 137; Jami Huisjen-Scott, page 153; Erik McGregor, page 164.

Publisher's Cataloging-In-Publication Data
Thistlethwaite, Susan Dr. Rev. #OccupytheBible: What Jesus Really Said (and Did) About Money and Power—1st ed.
Includes illustrations, photos, and endnotes

ISBN: 978-1-938231-44-5 (paperback)
ISBN: 978-1-938231-43-8 (epdf)
ISBN: 978-1-938231-42-1 (epub)

1. The Bible, theology and the current occupy Wall Street movement—2. Jesus of Nazareth; teaching and learning and knowledge—3. Religion and Faith—4. Money and power and the real message of Jesus Christ—5. The one percent versus the ninety-nine percent—6. American Christian Left wing and conservative politics and a new reading of the scriptures—I. Title

Book Design: Bookmasters

Jacket Cover Design: Ervin Serrano

Contents

Acknowledgments

MY MOST PROFOUND ACKNOWLEDGMENT MUST BE TO THE literally millions of people in nearly thirty countries around the world who have taken part in some form of an "Occupy" event. From the "Arab Spring" to the "*Indignados*" in Spain to the Occupy Wall Street movement and in many other places, people are refusing to be silent in the face of "austerity" measures that squeeze the poor and the middle class while those who caused a world-wide "Great Recession" have not been adequately held accountable.

The Spanish term "indignados," that is, those who are indignant at this state of affairs, is very revealing. It means those who are angry at something that is unjust or wrong. Our global economy has become ever more structurally unjust. The "Great Recession" has revealed this, but it is a condition that has been growing for a very long time. As ethicist Beverly Harrison so well said, "Anger is not the opposite of love. It is better understood as a feeling-signal that all is not well in our relation to other persons or groups or to the world around us. Anger is a mode of connectedness to others and is always a vivid form of caring."[1] She is right. All is very unwell in our economic relationships and we need to become more connected to that fact, not less. We must be angry enough and love enough to care.

I thank those who lift their voices, and place their feet and their hearts in the streets in order to make these unjust economic conditions visible. They give me great hope.

I would also like to acknowledge those who helped me more directly with this book. I would first like to thank the *Washington Post* online "On Faith" section, especially Sally Quinn, Editor-in-Chief of On Faith, for her vision and perseverance in creating that site. I would also like to thank Elizabeth Tenety, On Faith Editor, for some great dialogues and her wonderful eye for what photos to use to make a post really tell the story on multiple levels. I have first taken many of the ideas in this book out for a "test drive" in writing for "On Faith." I also want to acknowledge the *Washington Post* online for the permission to use what I have written for them under their guidelines.

My agent, Peter Rubie, certainly went the "second mile" (in biblical terms!) and not only found Astor + Blue Editions for me as a new and exciting publishing venture, but also read through the entire manuscript and made detailed edits and suggestions.

I would like to thank the generous photographers and designer groups who gave me permission to use their work gratis for this book. They are: Arturas Rosenbacher [We are the 1%], the American Values Network [Tea Party Jesus], Ilias Bartolini [Occupy Jesus], Timothy Krause [Chaos Sign], and Jami Huisjen-Scott [Dr. Thistlethwaite]. I would also like to thank all the photographers whose images I have included here for their artistry as I hope the photos help me tell this story more effectively.

I would like to thank my editorial assistant, Johnny Kline, who worked diligently to secure all these permissions and who also helped with the editorial process. Johnny also creatively turned statistics into a great chart to help tell the story of accelerating wealth, the decline of the middle class and accelerating poverty in the U.S.

There are intellectual debts as well that I would like to acknowledge. Dr. Sharon Ringe's fine work on the biblical understanding of the Jubilee was invaluable to me. Sharon is a great friend and a wonderful New Testament scholar. We worked together for many years on inclusive language biblical translations.

I must also acknowledge the debt of gratitude I feel toward my teacher of theology, Dr. Frederick Herzog, who taught me to measure our progress in discipleship by how we walked the walk. For Fred, it was never enough to just talk the talk.

I thank my wonderful and loving family, and especially my husband Dick, for their unwavering support for my work.

I dedicate this book to our grandchildren, and all children, that they may be able to live without fear and want in a world where love of neighbor has become the norm.

Introduction

". . . make a sanctuary [tent] for me, so that I may dwell among them."

(Exodus 25:8)

In 1932, twenty thousand men in tents occupied Washington DC, demanding a promised "bonus" for serving in World War I. The so-called Bonus Army was scattered with tear gas on orders from President Herbert Hoover.

BRING TENT

"Bring Tent" is the last line on the bottom of the original *Adbusters* poster promoting the start date of the occupation of Wall Street, September 17, 2011. The poster shows the iconic image of a ballerina dancing on top of the charging Wall Street bull.

This wasn't just an announcement of a rally. It was the announcement of an occupation.

The Internet group Anonymous encouraged its readers to join #OccupyWallStreet[2] calling protesters to "flood lower Manhattan, set up tents, kitchens, peaceful barricades and occupy Wall Street."[3] Like the #Jan25 Egyptian revolution in Tahrir Square, the Internet, and social media communications such as Twitter in particular, played an important role in the creation of the #Occupy movement and maintains a major role in its continuing influence. An Occupy Wall Street page on Facebook begun on September 19, 2011, showed a YouTube video of the earlier protests, and by September 22, the movement had reached critical mass.[4]

By mid-October, Facebook listed 125 #Occupy-related pages, and roughly one in every five hundred hash tags used on Twitter around the world was the movement's own #OWS.

Seemingly overnight, from L.A, to Chicago, to New York City, and south to Atlanta and Huston and beyond, Americans saw tents mushroom up in the midst of their towns and cities throughout the fall of 2011. The #Occupy movement began as a protest against the failure to prosecute bankers for causing the Great Recession and the undue influence of corporate money in politics. It had become a worldwide protest against the impoverishment and disenfranchisement of millions.

A TENT-DWELLING GOD

Tents are not speech, according to New York State Supreme Court Justice Michael Stallman, the judge who ruled against the continued occupation of Zuccotti Park in Lower Manhattan, where #Occupy first took root.[5] Tents, however impermanent, may be sacred nevertheless; indeed, in their wanderings in the wilderness, the Israelites met God in a tent built to God's specifications (See Exodus 25ff).

What kind of a God takes up residence in a tent so as to be with a people on the move? A journeying God. A God who is not fixed to one place, yet is known in a specific place—a tent-dwelling God. A God on the move combines the insights of religions that focus on the sacredness of place with those that emphasize the involvement of God in the events of human history.

The God of the Israelites was a wanderer, moving from place to place, not tied down. One striking thing we learn from these texts from ancient Israel is that although God is on the move, God is also found in a particular place. This seems contradictory, until you realize that, while you can take down a tent, pack it up and move it around, it is still a real structure and it occupies space. A "tent-dwelling God" is a movement God who nevertheless occupies a specific place. Location, therefore, is a very important way to begin to understand God's power for change and the positive changes of justice and mercy that the biblical prophets call for over and over.

Jesus of Nazareth stands in this biblical tradition—from Exodus to the prophets—as a Jewish reformer. In the first century CE, Jesus occupied very specific places, from Nazareth, to the Galilee, to Jerusalem, to Golgotha. Jesus related the places where he preached and taught, the places he occupied, to his Jewish scripture, and especially to the prophets.

Thus, the early Israelites, Jesus of Nazareth, and the #Occupy movement today occupy in more than one sense. Setting up a tent in a specific place, whether Zuccotti Park in New York City or the wilderness in the ancient Middle East, is one meaning of occupy. But "occupy" means more than "take up space." It also means to engage in a struggle to live out of a different reality, to not let yourself be defined by others but take back your own life, society, economy, and spiritual meaning from those who want to control you. To "occupy" also means to "take possession," and in the #Occupy movement that means to take back the definition of our own lives, our social relations, our economy, and indeed our spirituality from corporate interests that are gaining too much control over us in our democracy.

For the ancient Israelites, to occupy in the wilderness meant to escape slavery and then take possession of their own lives and follow their God, not Pharaoh. For Jesus of Nazareth, it meant living in the Kingdom of God right now, and not letting people be controlled by the Kingdom of Caesar or the Jewish Temple elites.

But those who want to control the society, and especially the economy, need to control the message. Moses had to get a message from God to go confront Pharaoh, and the biblical prophets kept calling on the Israelites to return to that message. Jesus did the same; he confronted those who were occupying the land of Israel, both literally, as the Romans did in their military occupation, and spiritually, as the Temple elites did with their narrow and legalistic interpretations of Jewish sacred texts.

Jesus not only literally occupied the rural and urban areas of his time with his followers as he moved around with large crowds following him, he also took back the interpretation of the sacred texts from those who were using the scripture, in his time, to justify driving people into poverty through increased debt and low wages, and driving them out of their homes and jobs.

Today, the #OccupyWallStreet movement is made up of people who are trying to literally take over space and live in it to make a statement about how they have been driven out of their homes and jobs by big banks and big corporations. They are not doing this just to make a political statement. They are trying to live in a way that makes the values of community and mutuality central, and to show what the common good looks like in practice.

The #Occupy movement has spread around the world, and people are constantly reinventing this form of protest from their own culture and history. In the United States, the #Occupy movement stands in the tradition of movements for peace and justice that have been part of American society for a very long time. In the "nation with the soul of a church,"[6] it is unsurprising that American social justice efforts often have had a distinctly religious bent. From opposition to slavery, to women agitating to get the vote, to the labor reforms of the Social Gospel, to the Civil Rights movement, to the movement to end violence against women, to the Farm Worker movement, religious faith has played a key role.

The #OccupyWallStreet movement stands both outside this tradition and within it. #Occupy began outside of the religious context altogether, but there has been tremendous interfaith religious involvement and support for the movement.

This book, however, asks a theological question: where is God when people #OccupyWallStreet? Different religions will answer that question differently. One way Christians can begin to answer it is to examine the key teachings of Jesus, especially on money and power. The teachings of Jesus as recorded in the Bible not only help us see the movement of God in history, but teach us how we need to act.

Right-wing Christianity would have you believe that the #Occupy movement, far from representing the divine presence on earth through calls to address economic inequality in our time, is driven by "a power of darkness," in other words, Satan.[7] Instead, they teach that the Bible is about personal salvation from a laundry list of what they deem individual "sins," such as homosexuality or using birth control. The first thing, therefore, that Christians must do if we are to understand what God is up to in our time is occupy our own sacred text.

BOOK OUTLINE

Tents are impermanent structures that move from place to place. But the key to occupying the Bible is location. Chapter 1 describes how to read the Bible from street level, and what happens when you move up to the eighth floor, like those who work at the Chicago Board of Trade. (Some inside the building put a sign in their eighth-floor windows that read, "We are the 1%.")

The Bible has been occupied before, by people on the streets all over the world. From Latin America, to Asia, to Africa, to Europe and the United States, people have read the Bible from the streets. In the United States, women who have been battered have read the Bible with black eyes and arms in a sling. African Americans, especially Dr. Martin Luther King, Jr., occupied the streets and occupied the Bible as well.

Many Americans, however, have not really made the fundamental connection between the Bible and economic justice. Wall Street has had a hand in many areas of life in our country, and surprisingly, biblical interpretation is one of them. This first chapter of this book explains how to #OccupytheBible in four steps. They're not easy steps, but they help us get along the road toward our prayer that God's will for justice and mercy be done "on earth as it is in heaven." You've got to actually get out on the streets and literally occupy a space for this way of reading the Bible to make sense. It's not the only thing you need to do, but it's a step you can't skip.

Chapter 2 is on temptation, and why temptation is always about the desire to gain power over others. The Devil will use every trick in the book to convince you that it's okay to want power, and that includes using scripture to make his point.

Few people seem to recognize that when Jesus is tempted in the wilderness (Matthew 4:1–11), he and the Devil are both trying to occupy scripture. They fling Deuteronomy and Psalms at each other, struggling over the meaning. Neither gains much ground by just quoting texts.

Then the Devil plays his trump card with temptation; he will give Jesus "all the kingdoms of the world and their splendor" if Jesus will just bow down and worship him.

The gloves are off. That's what occupying sacred texts really comes down to, isn't it? A struggle for power. Satan, as the tempter, is the one who knows this, and knows it well. He will just tempt Jesus to reach out now for political power over all the kingdoms of the world (and how much the Devil reveals about the demonic nature of absolute political power in that verse!) and he'll control Jesus.

Jesus resists. Resisting the temptation of absolute power is crucial to occupying sacred texts. Power always wants more, always wants to tempt you to overreach—and that's how Jesus triumphs over the Devil. He won't play.

So much of American life is tied up in wrestling with the temptation to overreach, to think of ourselves as exceptional and not resist the lure of political and financial power.

Chapter 3, "Den of Thieves," focuses on what Jesus did when he occupied the Temple in Jerusalem. "Then Jesus entered the temple and drove out all who were selling and buying in the temple, and he overturned the tables of the money changers . . ." (Matthew 21:12).

When Jesus drove the moneychangers out of the Temple in Jerusalem, he took on the brokers who were ripping off the pilgrims who came during Passover. These brokers (bankers) were in cahoots with the priestly class who ran the Temple, and together they would cheat pilgrims out of the just price of their offerings. The bankers would sell their own Temple coinage in exchange for foreign money, charging interest on the transaction.

The Temple in Jerusalem was in a sense the national bank of Israel in Jesus' time; it was a powerful national treasury that did not let its great wealth sit idle. The bank lent the money it collected at interest, violating Jewish tradition on lending, especially lending to the poor. These unjust lending practices drove many residents into extreme poverty and created the vast number of slum dwellers of Jerusalem.

When you #OccupytheBible on money, this text is where you need to start. There is a prophetic tradition in the Hebrew Bible that prohibits the charging of interest, especially to the poor, or severely limits it. Jesus is drawing on this prophetic teaching to challenge these unfair lending practices.

Our current economic crisis is really a credit crisis generated by the way banks decided to change their lending practices, effectively crashing the system.

In Chapter 4 I examine not only how Jesus occupied, but also how he engaged downtrodden workers by calling some of them to be his disciples. John Dominic Crossan, in his wonderful book *God and Empire: Jesus Against Rome Then and Now,* asks us to consider why Jesus of Nazareth would walk all the way to Galilee (Mark 1:16) to begin his ministry when he could just as easily have done so closer to home. And why seek out all these fishermen? Why is Jesus systematically recruiting people who fish to be his disciples?

Crossan points out that the Roman imperial project of over-commercialization of the fishing industry took place during the time of Jesus. Herod Antipas regulated the indigenous fishing industry around the Sea of Galilee and took it pretty much out of profitability right around the time of Jesus.

These formerly prosperous fishing families were now scraping to keep their boats and their lives together under the ruinous economic practices of Imperial Rome. Crossan argues that Jesus wanted to call as disciples those who would understand the stark difference between his teaching that "the kingdom of God is in your midst" and the kingdom of Caesar being forced on the Jews by imperial Rome. Antipas began to "commercialize the lake [Sea of Galilee] and its fishers in the name of Rome's empire and both John and Jesus clashed with him in the name of Israel's God."[8]

Jesus recruits people who will "get it" to be his disciples. The core of his message is that the Kingdom of Herod Antipas and the Kingdom of God are clashing right now, in human history, and people need to take sides, against or for the justice and mercy of God's message. Men who had just been put out of work or nearly out of business by the rule of Rome were standing around on the shore in Galilee mending worn-out nets, worrying about whether their patched-up boats would survive a storm. These are the people, in Jesus' recruitment strategy, who could hear the message he was preaching because they were being crushed down by Roman occupation. The poor fishers would be better able to occupy another message and understand why following Jesus meant resisting Rome.

Chapter 5 is about how Jesus taught in parables as a way to contrast the Kingdom of God and the Kingdom of Herod Antipas and his collaborators. The parables of the Talents and of the Workers in the Vineyard are paired because they involve money and wealth accumulation, both through investing and in owning land. While the parables are told in individual Gospel accounts to help people in those communities understand their location, the location of Jesus as he walked around Israel, teaching from Judaea to the Galilee, must also be taken into account in relation to our location on the streets today. The people from the fields or on the streets who came to listen to Jesus were most likely those suffering from unjust economic practices, but that doesn't mean they could articulate or clearly understand what was wrong. Parables are dramas of reversal, where folks are suddenly in a crisis in the making and have to choose where they will stand.

In Chapter 6, I examine Jesus' economic plan, the Jubilee. God commands Moses to observe a "Jubilee," a holy year where the community's balance sheet would be straightened out. In the year of Jubilee, debts would be forgiven and lands returned to their rightful owners. In the year of Jubilee, any Jew enslaved by another would be set free. During this holy year, injustice would be righted, oppression would cease, and the people would experience safety and fruitfulness in their land. This is the "good news" that Jesus announces as he starts his ministry. He reads from Jubilee scripture, Isaiah 61, and announces his plan. "Today, this scripture has been fulfilled in your hearing" (Luke 4:18–19). Jesus does have an economic model, and it's not free market (i.e., unregulated) capitalism. Jesus' economic plan is about sharing resources and celebrating community. This kind of economic model is about "power with" not "power over."

Chapter 7 begins a series of chapters that take an even closer look at power. Gender is always a subject for the exercise of power as control, and in this chapter I examine how Jesus valued women's leadership and even trained a woman, Mary Magdalene, to be an apostle. In the New Testament, Mary Magdalene was healed by Jesus, she supported his movement financially, and she was one of the last of his followers at the cross and the first to speak to him after his resurrection. In the Gnostic text "The Gospel of Mary," newly discovered with other such extra-biblical texts in the nineteenth century, Mary Magdalene appears as a disciple, singled out by Jesus for special teachings. She is portrayed as being in a struggle for leadership of the Jesus movement, especially with Peter, after Jesus' ascension.[9] Mary Magdalene was venerated by members of the early church, but in the late sixth century CE, the hierarchy attacked her. Pope Gregory identified her, with no evidence from the New Testament, as a prostitute. This woman of power in the Jesus movement was apparently too powerful, and she was sexually shamed by the church. But in modern times, women have been occupying scripture since the suffrage movement, and their biblical insights help illumine how Jesus' understanding of power and economic equality includes gender.

Sexual shaming of women continues into the twenty-first century, however, as witnessed in 2012 with the controversy surrounding radio personality Rush Limbaugh and his attacks on Sandra Fluke, a Georgetown University student who attempted to testify about women's need for healthcare contraceptive coverage. Women, and their male allies, successfully pushed back at Limbaugh, indicating a new era in how we think about women and power. But #OWS has not always been a safe space for women, and more work is needed in the movement to include gender in all its facets, including race and class. The fact that Jesus of Nazareth respected women's leadership, as shown in his teaching, healing, and friendship with Mary Magdalene, is another way to understand how power for economic and social change needs to be exercised today.

Chapter 8 exposes the fundamental weakness of power exercised as violence as seen in the crucifixion of Jesus of Nazareth by the Romans. The weakness of power as cruel violence can also be seen in the decisions by the Bush administration to engage in torture, and it flags an increasing danger in the United States today with the militarization of police forces that pose a danger to democracy.

Chapter 9 explains how to reverse the dynamic of "power over" and turn it into "power with" by a deeper reading of the Sermon on the Mount and Jesus' teaching that when we do not care for the "least of these"—the hungry, the homeless poor, and the prisoner—we are also failing to care for him. To fully understand Jesus' message today, however, we have to occupy the Apocalypse, that is, take back the meaning of God's judgment from the Christian Right. Instead of realizing that Jesus' message about judgment is about what we do here and now, the Christian Right has focused on a coming Rapture, where the true believers will go right up to heaven, and the rest of us will be "left behind."

The real message of Jesus today, however, is that the poor and the middle class are the ones being "left behind" in this economy, and the real Apocalypse—the crushing amount of debt accumulated by two wars and a big tax cut for the rich—is already upon us. We need to occupy the Apocalypse in order to take back the real message of Jesus on judgment in the here and now.

The conclusion asks Christians to consider whether the church can be a new location for the #Occupy message. The answer is both yes and no. #OWS is a secular and interreligious movement, and it is not and should not be synonymous with the church. But #Occupy can be a sign to the institutional church of where it needs to engage in our time, and how the church needs to #OccupytheBible to find a way to both talk the talk of what Jesus really said, and walk the walk of what Jesus really did.

A MOVEMENT JESUS

Jesus of Nazareth moved around quite a bit. He was an itinerant preacher and healer, someone whose feet were dirty and sore from travel. Sometimes Jesus didn't even have a tent and had nowhere to lay his head.

Jesus occupied. He organized fishers whose industry was being destroyed by Rome. He occupied a bank. One of his closest friends and one of his students, a person whom he trusted to carry on his ministry, was a powerful woman. Jesus did street theater and the Romans killed him as a dangerous criminal. His life, death, and resurrection are a judgment on the abuses of top-down forms of power that lend privilege to the wealthy and crush the poor.

The Bible today has been captured by the "ownership" crowd, those who side with the empire of money and power, and they are co-opting the Bible to serve the purposes of money and power. In America, the Christian Right has made Jesus into the kind of capitalist who spurns regulation, and this book is about showing that this view is simply untrue to the biblical text.

We have seen this all before. The "robber barons" of the nineteenth century created hell on earth for the majority of Americans with unsafe working conditions, long hours, no safety regulations, child labor, no healthcare, no safety net for the elderly, and exploitation of women workers. Church officials of the time, both Protestant and Catholic, either helped the power elite or did nothing to stop them.

But there were also those who resisted the machinations of big money and power. Long before #Occupy, the Populists, the People's Party, "exploded on the American scene and quickly faded, though its platform did not. After years of ferment and debate, the party made what were once considered radical demands. It called for a progressive income tax, some form of social security, workplace regulation, banking regulation. It sought the secret ballot and direct election of senators. The hard-core Populists remained on the fringes, shouting to be heard, refusing to be co-opted, holding fast to their dream of a cooperative commonwealth. Yet much of what they envisioned came to pass within 40 years of the party's flameout in the 1890s."[10]

The Social Gospel, as well as a social justice–minded Catholicism exemplified by the work of Father John Ryan, supported these reforms, helped provide them with a biblical and moral platform in the early twentieth century, and moved them forward. We have had a social safety net, as well as a thriving middle class, in this country thanks to both labor movements and Christian witness of principled religious people who joined with them.

And these very reforms are now under systematic attack yet again. It is once again time to occupy and to do so with a new Social Gospel reading of the Bible, the insights of Catholic Social teaching, the *Tikkun olam* (repairing the world) of Judaism, the Ramadan spirit of Islam, and all the religious insight that people of faith and people of humanist values have gained from the street. In fact, this occupation is long overdue.

1

Reading the Bible from the Streets

LOCATION, LOCATION, LOCATION

The Chicago Board of Trade is the world's oldest futures and options exchange, currently housed in a 1930s-style building on West Jackson Boulevard in Chicago. Eight stories above street level, a sign appeared in the windows overlooking the streets where #Occupy demonstrators were marching in Chicago.

It boasted, "We are the 1%."[11]

Location is everything, and not only in real estate. The view of human life and its meaning from eight stories up in Chicago's oldest mercantile exchange is very different than at street level, where protestors walk.

Occupying the Bible first means knowing your location. If you are located eight stories up and work at trading financial instruments, in effect betting on what will happen with money (equities and currencies) or food (commodities), your view will be shaped by this work. Here's what can happen. What if your

Chicago Board of Trade windows display "We Are The 1%" signs during Occupy protests in Chicago, Illinois.
Arturas Rosenbacher, October 2011

best bet is that there will be food shortages due to bad weather (and yes, there is even trading at the Merc on weather!). You will try to corner the market on certain foods, driving up the price. When food prices rise, your profit will enable you to be even better fed than you are today, regardless of the increased hunger you may have helped create at street level. Location can matter very much, even to whether you eat or not.

Interpreting the Bible from street level isn't a theory. It must, without exception, start with the physical: the location and condition of human bodies. Gustavo Gutierrez, a pioneer of reading the Bible from the perspective of those at street level rather than those on the eighth floor, once explained the importance of understanding theology from the most human of locations, the body. Gutierrez was being honored at a faculty reception at a school where he was a visiting professor. There was a lavish buffet, and a senior professor in theology, carrying a plate piled high with food from the buffet, came over to where Gutierrez and I were chatting. He loomed over

Gutierrez and intoned, "So, Professor Gutierrez, explain liberation theology to me."

Gutierrez looked at him for a moment and replied, "It's a matter of the stomach."

"The stomach?" the tall, portly professor said.

"Yes," said Gutierrez. He looked pointedly at the professor's loaded plate. "You do theology differently when your stomach is full than when it is empty."[12]

Those who are on the street, who are hungry and in poor health, are the ones feeling the real effects of economic policies that have made *half* of all Americans poor or near poor, according to new Census Bureau data.[13] They are located closer to the truth of what's going on in our country today than those up on the eighth floor. It really is a matter of location.

Of course, wealth isn't evil in itself. But wealth often becomes a barrier to actually feeling the consequences of your actions, such as seeing the world from the perspective of someone who has an empty stomach rather than a full one. In the biblical teachings of Jesus, as we will see, wealth becomes a stumbling block, a barrier to getting clear on God's reign of justice and mercy. Wealth allows you to hide from what's really going on at ground level. Wealth persuades you that you deserve special treatment; it gives a false sense of entitlement and tends, as a recent study shows, to make you less compassionate. Ironically, those who have less, this same study demonstrates, share more.[14]

I'm saying, really, that there's no neutral location, no place to just stand by, in this way of approaching the Bible. Occupying the Bible means taking a stand, literally. How you interpret what the Bible means is very much determined by your location and the actions you take in that location. If you have financial means and occupy the eighth floor, location means your wealth determines how you interpret the Bible. However, in standing with those who have less, you are acting differently, and this means you can see things differently.

For those at street level, who have relatively little, the challenge is realizing your struggles are not just about you, they are about all those who are like you. Those on the street also need to really see what the Bible is talking about when it comes to wealth and poverty, power and powerlessness. It's just that those on the street have less standing in the way of their understanding that biblical message.

A lot of misunderstanding about interpreting the Bible has come from the street level, from the "underside" as Mary Potter Engel and I describe it in *Lift Every Voice: Constructing Christian Theology from the Underside.*[15] Despite the continuing use of *Lift Every Voice* since 1990 in theological classrooms across the United States and around the world, really reading the Bible from the street—what has been called "liberation theology"—has not caught on much in either theological academies or mainline churches. Its influence has been marginal because classrooms and most churches have little or no connection to the street. Thus, until recently, study of the Bible in the United States in particular, especially for those on the underside, has rarely informed an awareness of the connection between money and power and social justice.

That is changing. The dramatic increase in the wealth of the 1% and the relative deprivation of the other 99%, so well documented in the fall 2011 report from the Congressional Budget Office on changes in income from 1979 to the present,[16] has created a new consensus among a large majority of Americans on the need to address income inequality not only as an economic issue, but as a moral issue.

The data grouping on the following chart has become famous; it has been used on television news shows and on many signs at #Occupy rallies. This is the state of America after thirty years of conservative economic policies that favor the rich over the rest:

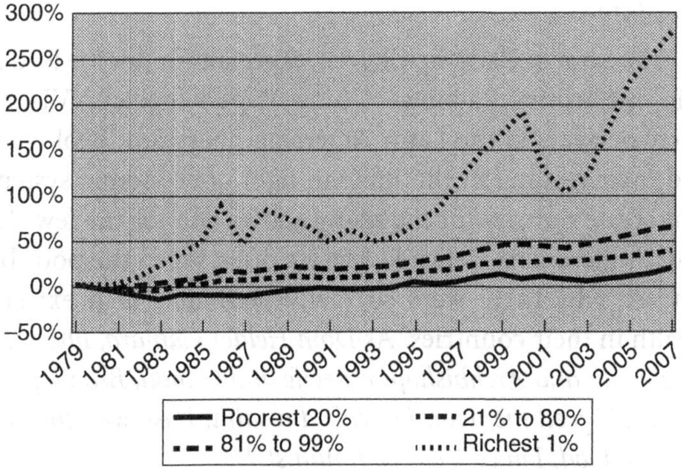

Statistics from the Congressional Budget Office show how incomes for the top 1% have soared in comparison to everyone else.

Congressional Budget Office, October 25, 2011

This chart shows what the #OccupyWallStreet protests have been about. The location of most Americans is at the bottom of the pile, while a very few sit on the top.

WALL STREET RULES ON BIBLICAL INTERPRETATION

But it's not going to be easy to #OccupytheBible. Wall Street has not only dominated the American economy. Curiously enough, it has dominated interpretation of the Bible as well. There is fear and loathing among the powerful and their apologists regarding reading the Bible from the streets, from the perspective of the poor and the powerless. And so far, the Wall Street rules have been successful in stomping on such biblical interpretation, not only in the United States, but also around the world.

The Roman Catholic Church, especially under the leadership of Cardinal Ratzinger[17] (now Pope Benedict XVI), actively persecuted the Latin American liberation theologians and their reading of the Bible in light of economic systems that create poverty for the many and wealth for the few. The church hierarchy preferred that its priests feed the poor but not ask why there were so many poor and such extreme wealth in their countries. *As Dom Helder Camara, liberation theologian and Archbishop of Recife and Olinda, Brazil, put it so well, "I feed the poor, I'm called a saint. I ask why the poor have no food, I'm called a communist."*[18]

Similarly, far right–wing American Christians have frequently attacked efforts to interpret the Bible as siding with the poor and the oppressed, especially when this has included a social and economic critique. They have condemned both historical and contemporary approaches to liberation theology as Marxism, as seen, for example, in a "Summit Ministries" video.[19] Glenn Beck, the television and radio personality and Mormon convert, has continued this theme in his diatribes against "liberation theology" as "Marxism disguised as religion."[20]

The problem is, as I have pointed out many times, despite Glenn Beck's fulminating against interpreting the Bible from below, the early church was unquestionably socialist.[21]

The Acts of the Apostles makes this crystal clear:

> *Now the whole group of those who believed were of one heart and soul, and no one claimed private ownership of any possessions, but everything they owned was held in common. With great power the apostles gave their testimony to the resurrection of the Lord Jesus, and great grace was upon them all. There was not a needy person among them, for as many as owned lands or houses sold them and brought the proceeds of what was sold. They laid it at the apostles' feet, and it was distributed to each as any had need. (4:32–35)*

The apostles' way of holding what they had in common is more like democratic socialism than it is like the Soviet collectivist model, heaven knows. A literal reading of the Acts of the Apostles in the New Testament, so often favored by conservative-thinking Christians like Beck, does not allow for any other interpretation than that the early church was working from a proto-socialist model. Democratic socialism favors worker cooperation and worker ownership of the means of production, rather than ownership by the state. But democratic socialism has also come to mean a large social safety net so that people who are in need get taken care of directly, *just like the early church did.*

Progressive Evangelicals like Rev. Jim Wallis know that the struggle for the Bible on the issues of wealth and poverty is all-important. In his many books, sermons, and articles, Wallis has consistently argued that social justice is a faith-based commitment to serve the poor and to change the conditions that lead to so much poverty, and that these are central tenets of the teachings of Jesus that lie at the heart of biblical faith. In Wallis' book *Rediscovering Our Values: On Wall Street, Main Street, and Your Street,*[22] he makes a cogent argument that greed and inequality are biblically wrong, and economically unsound. It is far from a radical book, but Wallis has been attacked relentlessly for bringing up money as a Christian issue by the likes of conservatives such as Glenn Beck. The idea that Christianity provides a critique of capitalism is anathema to conservatives, as seen in book-length critiques such as Jay W. Richards's *Money, Greed, and God: Why Capitalism Is the Solution Not the Problem.*[23] Richards is a senior fellow at the conservative Acton Institute and is best known for his advocacy of intelligent design, that is, creationism, an anti-evolutionary thesis.

Jim Wallis often talks about Jesus and the poor and how we treat them in our society as a biblical priority. Wallis is one of the few religious writers read by religious progressives and mainline Christians who discuss wealth and poverty. Marcus Borg and John Shelby Spong, the biblical interpreters who are most often read by religious progressives, do not primarily pursue a strong economic critique. They have worked extensively on biblical interpretation, especially in a search for the historical Jesus, but not primarily through an economic lens.

In today's broken economy, the word of scripture on economic justice is the word we most need to hear and heed for the well-being of our bodies, minds, and spirits.

The most important point we need to keep in mind is that we cannot deeply understand the teachings of Jesus on money or power, unless we are engaged in movements that try to occupy that message, that is, to engage it in deeds as well as words.

BATTERED WOMEN OCCUPY THE BIBLE

In 1981, I published an article in the journal *Christianity and Crisis* called "The Bible and Battered Women: From Subjection to Liberation."[24] It was based on years of Bible study with women who had been—and some who still were—beaten by their husbands or partners.

These Bible studies started when I was a local church pastor in Durham, North Carolina, in the 1970s. At that time, I helped start a local hotline for women in crisis. Women would call and say, "I want to talk to the pastor," and I would take the call. Our telephone conversations often began with the words, "I'm a Bible-believing Christian, but . . ." and then the women would proceed to tell me how their husbands were hitting them. I brought some of these women together to form Bible study groups, and I continued this practice when I moved to Massachusetts.

I learned from these women how to read the Bible from below. They would come to study the Bible with black eyes, an arm in a sling, or a cautious manner that spoke of years of expecting a slap or blow if they spoke. They wanted to know, simply, does God give my husband permission to hit me? I combed the scriptures for texts for them to read; I brought texts that showed how much Jesus honored women and women's leadership (Mary and Martha), how women were also disciples (Mary Magdalene), and how Jesus told the disciples that if their gifts were not honored, they should "shake off the dust from your feet" and get out. All that was necessary was for these battered women to really *read and hear* the Gospel message of love of God and neighbor, of Jesus' defense of the woman taken in adultery, of the discipleship of women.

And suddenly, they saw and they heard and they knew that this violence against them was not God's plan, but human sin. They saw what the text really said because of their location as the beaten, the despised, and the lost whom Jesus came to find.

I didn't invent this way of reading the Bible. These battered women taught it to me as they struggled to find guidance in scripture that would allow them some freedom from violence. They were struggling against their church, and their husbands, who often used scripture such as "wives be subject to your husbands" to justify the beatings.

From these battered women, I learned to be suspicious[25] even of my own Protestant tradition, which was supposed to be rooted in "protest" against ecclesial authority, which took away individuals' ability to understand scripture. When the Protestant dissenters broke from the Roman Catholic Church, they claimed a "priesthood of all believers." This meant in principle that each believer could go directly to God, and by extension to the sacred texts, and directly experience the sacred without the mediation of church or priest. This was held to be the work of the Holy Spirit.

But the Bible study I've learned from battered women is equally subversive of the approved Protestant readings of scripture that have developed since the Reformation. Though in theory Protestants claim a spirit-led equality of Bible reading, in practice Protestant authorities have often tried to clamp down on what they regarded as excesses of the spirit. Martin Luther once complained about a man who seemed to him to "have swallowed the Holy Spirit, feathers and all."

The spirit is notoriously hard to control. Since the sixteenth century, certain readings of scripture and certain religious practices have become acceptable to Protestants, and other interpretations, no matter how much the interpreter might claim to be guided by the Holy Spirit, have been regarded as suspect or even heretical.

The full equality of women, including their equality in marriage and in society, is still heretical. But it is deeply, deeply affirmed in the life and ministry of Jesus of Nazareth.

My article on the Bible and battered women is used all over the world and is more quoted and reproduced than anything else I have written.[26] It has become part of the literature of reading the Bible from below that developed in the second half of the twentieth century. During this period, not only priests like Gutierrez but also ordinary Christians from around the world, and especially women, began to read the Bible with new eyes. In South Africa, Asia, and Latin America, these Christians read the Bible from below and let it speak directly to their exploited and desperate situations. Some of those who read with new eyes were Protestants, and some were Catholics responding to the invitation of Vatican II to read the Bible themselves and not leave it to the priests to tell them what the Bible said.

These ordinary Christians have already occupied the Bible.

NOBODY OCCUPIED THE BIBLE BETTER THAN DR. MARTIN LUTHER KING, JR.

The African American church tradition has long been rooted in reading from below, as is evident in the remarkable works of enslaved Africans. These slaves took the white missionary preaching and turned it to their own liberation. The white-approved "slaves obey your earthly masters" was transformed into "exodus." This was a communal work, though it was hidden from the white clergy.

The movement was neither linear nor easy; African American believers and their churches are diverse in their approaches to the Bible. But there is a remarkable history in the African American community of reading the Bible from below, from the location of slavery, Jim and Jane Crow, and continued assaults on the full equality of African Americans.[27] There is a consistent use of the Bible to resist white racist deformation of black identity, to help make a way out of no way in the face of economic and social deprivation, and to use the Bible as a resource to help create social change.

And no one in the history of reading the Bible from the streets was better at it than Dr. Martin Luther King, Jr. The fundamental concept Dr. King understood is that you have to be on the street to read the Bible from the street. As Rev. Jesse Jackson once said to me, "All these people getting PhDs in the work of Dr. King, and not one of them could call a press conference." It's true. Dr. King could call the press conference, stand up on a podium, and say what really needed to be said, and the dozens, then hundreds, then hundreds of thousands of people who stood with him on the street could say the same. When Dr. King marched, a multi-religious, multi-racial America suddenly became visible, and America was forever changed.

Dr. King was no biblical literalist. He was more concerned with how to get people to be less preoccupied with creeds and more focused on deeds. In fact, he believed, the job of the church and its scriptures was "to produce living witnesses

The Rev. Dr. Martin Luther King, Jr. marches with rabbis, priests, and pastors at Arlington National Cemetery.
© John C. Goodwin, Feb. 6, 1968, CALCAV march, Arlington Cemetery (Clergy and Laymen Concerned about Vietnam), February 6, 1968

and testimonies to the power of God in human experience,"[28] and to commit to action. "Jesus," he noted, "always recognized that there is a danger of having a high blood pressure of creeds and an anemia of deeds."[29]

Martin Luther King, Jr. was all about deeds. This is why, in his famous "I Have a Dream" speech, he was able to move so deftly between "the unalienable rights of life, liberty, and the pursuit of happiness" declared in the Declaration of Independence and the words of the prophet Isaiah:

> *I have a dream that one day every valley shall be exalted, every hill and mountain shall be made low, the rough*

places will be made plain, and the crooked places will be made straight, and the glory of the Lord shall be revealed, and all flesh shall see it together.[30]

And then came the deeds part: the words of the founders and of scripture, no matter how inspiring according to Dr. King, must lead to a concrete change in the attitudes and laws "down in Alabama, with its vicious racists." Otherwise, the words are a promissory note that has been returned in default.

From the perspective of the streets, where Dr. King marched, loving one's enemies was the only practical way. This is elaborated in his extraordinary sermon on Jesus' teaching in the Sermon on the Mount in Matthew 5:43ff.[31] It demonstrates how Dr. King interpreted the Bible from the streets in order to turn words into deeds.

In this sermon, Dr. King took as his text the words of Jesus, "You have heard that it was said, 'Love your neighbor and hate your enemy.' But I tell you, love your enemies and pray for those who persecute you . . ."

Dr. King argued in this sermon that when Jesus said, "love your enemies" he was talking about the secret of the power of nonviolent action.

There is a power in love that our world has not discovered yet. Jesus discovered it centuries ago. Mahatma Gandhi of India discovered it a few years ago, but most men and most women never discover it. For they believe in hitting for hitting; they believe in an eye for an eye and a tooth for a tooth; they believe in hating for hating; but Jesus comes to us and says, "This isn't the way."[32]

As Dr. King's concludes in his sermon, and as he demonstrated in his words and his deeds, what works to overcome hate is "to organize mass non-violent resistance based on the principle of love." This is exactly what #OccupyWallStreet has been trying to do. It's ultimately why those who want to make a change in this country have got to get out on the streets.

POWER COMES FROM THE STREET

Nonviolent direct action is one of the most effective discoveries of the twentieth century in terms of how power is actually distributed in a society. From Mohandas Gandhi in India to Dr. King in the United States, the secret of the power of nonviolence is that it comes from below.

The discovery of the real nature of power in society and the specifics of how to create change from the streets is best analyzed in the work of Gene Sharp. Through in-depth studies of the work of Gandhi and others, Sharp has provided a pragmatic political analysis of the use of power through nonviolence. His work is considered a classic, has been translated into many languages, and is used all over the world in creating nonviolent change, from Asia to the Middle East and in the United States.[33]

Sharp's key theme is that power does not come from the top and filter down, nor is it a possession of those in charge. For Sharp, political power—the power of any state, regardless of its particular structure—ultimately derives from the subjects of the state. Authorities rule with the implicit consent of those ruled, whether this consent is given by choice or taken under threat. Thus, Sharp's fundamental insight is that any power structure relies on the subjects' obedience to the orders of the ruler(s) to survive. If subjects do not obey, leaders lose their power.

This power of nonviolence is nearly unstoppable when citizens learn how to exercise and deploy it by withdrawing this consent.

This is the truth force that nonviolent activists from the southern tip of Manhattan to the northern boundaries of Seattle have learned by getting to know our society from below. The truth that is now coming into focus, for Wall Street and for Main Street, through these street-level protests, is the systemic violence of the American economy today on the majority of its citizens. Our economy produces riskier and riskier financial instruments and fewer and fewer decent jobs. The Great Recession, a direct result of the reckless financial

A huge throng of Occupy protestors marching in lower Manhattan near Wall Street.

Mario Tama/Getty Images News, October 5, 2011

practices of Wall Street, has driven many into poverty and threatens the viability of the American middle class.

Dr. King is memorialized now in Washington, DC. But his greatest memorial is when people actually follow his example by reading the Bible from the street and acting on the teachings of the biblical prophets and Jesus of Nazareth on money and power.

Of the fourteen inscriptions on the wall of the new King memorial, this one seems particularly apt for the economic struggles of today:

> *I have the audacity to believe that peoples everywhere can have three meals a day for their bodies, education and culture for their minds, and dignity, equality and freedom for their spirits. (10 December 1964, Oslo, Norway)*

The lesson of battered women who read the Bible with new eyes, the civil rights movement in addressing institutional racism, the #Occupy movement, and many other movements is that power resides on the street. But demonstrations are not enough; the power of the street needs to become visible.

#OCCUPY SOCIAL MEDIA

As Gandhi used the newsreel to influence opinion for his nonviolent work in India, Dr. King used the new media of his time, especially television, to great effect. Televised images of police dogs and fire hoses being used against peaceful demonstrators generated a national outcry against the strong-arm tactics of the segregationists, such as those in Birmingham,

Alabama, and this influenced President Kennedy to introduce major civil rights legislation.[34]

Today's new social media not only makes sharing videos and pictures of human rights violations and economic injustice easier, it is also interactive and proactive. Social media makes the individual into a creator of media, not just the passive recipient of news generated by others. This may be its most significant impact. Anyone with a cell phone camera can now make media that can influence political events.

Social media and street demonstrations have this in common: people stop feeling passive in the face of injustice and take action. This is the most fundamental change of all: human beings realize that they can become agents in history, not just pawns of the powerful. Mary Potter Engel, my co-author and co-editor of *Lift Every Voice*, once remarked, "The most powerful question you can ask is 'who the hell set things up this way?'" Once you start questioning the idea that things have to be the way they are, you are on the road to making history as an agent for change.

Thus, while Facebook, Twitter, and other social media are great for organizing demonstrations, their greatest power is that they all engage people in creative work in order to effect that change. Social media is not a substitute for actually getting out in the streets to demonstrate, but as #Jan25, the Egyptian Facebook revolution, and #OccupyWallStreet have shown, social media activism can fuel street activism, and street activism can lead to new media.

The "Tea Party Jesus: Sermon on the Mall" YouTube video made by TeaPartyJesus.org features a cartoon Jesus who changes the Sermon on the Mount into the words of the Tea Party platform, with pithy preaching such as:

Tea Party Jesus cartoon features Ayn Rand, Glenn Beck, Sarah Palin, Rick Perry, Newt Gingrich, Rick Santorum, Paul Ryan, Rush Limbaugh, Michele Bachmann, and Mitt Romney as Jesus' disciples. www.teapartyjesus.org

American Values Network, December 8, 2011

"Blessed are those who hunger and thirst for lower taxes."

"Blessed are those who follow my prophet, Ayn Rand."

"Blessed are the pure in ideology."[35]

At the end, the cartoon shifts to a different Jesus preaching the actual words of the Sermon on the Mount. This is a wonderful example of how to creatively occupy new media and #OccupytheBible.

HOW TO #OCCUPYTHEBIBLE

We can learn several important lessons in how to #OccupytheBible from these examples.

• ***First, get to know the Bible.*** The whole Bible. When police raided Zuccotti Park and destroyed many of the belongings of the #Occupiers, one of the major areas of destruction was the People's Library. Bibles lay in the heap alongside books by Maya Angelou, Stephen King, and J. K. Rowling, all marked with the People's Library stamp.[36] While many households and #Occupy camps have Bibles, actually reading it is essential. As studies have shown, people become more liberal in their social attitudes by actually reading the Bible, especially on their own—that is, outside of church teaching.[37]

This is why the Bible is where the action is in the conservative/progressive social and economic struggle in the United States today. In fact, conservatives are working on a Conservative Bible Project to cut out passages considered too liberal from the Bible and also to change wording.[38]

So, read the Bible, but be sure to get a New Revised Standard Version.

• ***Second, get out on the street.*** There's no substitute for this. Without putting yourself where people are gathering to discuss their specific economic and social plight and where they are acting together to demonstrate for a different kind of America, you can't get it. We need an America where inequality is considered a major problem by both political parties and concrete legislative reforms are adopted and implemented that regulate banking practices, reduce corporate influence in politics, raise the minimum wage, reform lending to students, provide for universal healthcare, and establish incentives for creating and keeping jobs in the United States. This isn't all we need, by a long shot, but it is a very good start. That's why conservative resistance to these changes is so very strong.

• ***Third, use social media.*** Social media strengthens movements for change in many ways. It is great for organizing demonstrations, as people who use social media can be empowered and inclined to take another step in activism, police abuses can be documented and challenged, new ideas can be circulated, and attacks on movements to challenge the role of money and power in politics can be effectively critiqued.

It is especially important to use social media to challenge the way religious and political conservatives use the Bible to justify their economic and social policies. When someone argues that "God is the invisible hand behind the market," that statement needs to be immediately engaged publically, and informed biblical and theological critiques must be used to offer another perspective. As biblical values have been a cornerstone of the movement of American religion and politics to the Right in the last three decades, biblical values will be a crucial part of moving us 180 degrees in the other direction.

• ***Fourth, make the connections.*** Many people read the Bible, demonstrate in support of economic equality, and creatively use social media, but these experiences must talk to each other. The texts of scripture come from many different people trying to make sense of God's vision of human wholeness and well-being and how to live up to it over a long period of time and understand it in their communities. We should not fall into a liberal or progressive fundamentalism just to counter right-wing fundamentalism.

The teachings of Jesus, for example, aren't in the form of YouTube videos. They are what the earliest Christians remembered about Jesus and what he taught, and they brought those teachings into their own communities and asked themselves what difference those teachings made for their own lives. That's why we have four Gospels, not just one. Each community brought the teachings into their lives in different ways.

We experience our communities in different ways today. Just because people call themselves "the 99%" doesn't mean they all agree. The real differences among the majority of Americans in class, race, gender, sexual orientation, age, national origin, and a host of other conditions set us as much in conflict as in agreement on the ways to address inequality. Addressing these differences in a transformative way is long overdue. This, too, is part of the experience of the streets. It was part of the experience of Zuccotti Park, where people of different races, ethnicities, and educational levels camped in different places, and violence against women occurred. The experience of the street is an experience of conflict and confusion and that has to be central to how we #OccupytheBible. To pretend that everybody is united and in harmony is a betrayal of the many sources of pain in our society.

Isn't that the principle of what #OWS calls the "Assembly"? It is an open-mic method that lets everyone who wants to have a say in the decision-making. When it comes to #OccupytheBible, the more diversity the better. This is the difference getting out on the street can make in how we read the Bible. Those who put up signs reading "We are the 1%" in their eighth-floor windows at the Chicago Mercantile Exchange did not take the time to walk down to street level and hear the concerns of the #Occupy protestors. They stayed among their fellow workers, and their own privilege was reinforced. By contrast, one of the great strengths of the

Civil Rights movement was the diversity of the people who marched with Dr. King, both supporting the movement and learning along the way what racial prejudice really was when you looked it in the eye at close range. Physically changing your perspective helps you realize the deep meaning of what Jesus taught as he walked among the people.

2

Temptation: It's All About Power

THE TEMPTATION OF JESUS

Then Jesus was led up by the Spirit into the wilderness to be tempted by the Devil. He fasted forty days and forty nights, and afterwards he was famished. The tempter came and said to him, "If you are the Son of God, command these stones to become loaves of bread." But he answered, "It is written, 'One does not live by bread alone, but by every word that comes from the mouth of God.'" Then the Devil took him to the holy city and placed him on the pinnacle of the temple, saying to him, "If you are the Son of God, throw yourself down; for it is written, 'He will command his angels concerning you,' and 'On their hands they will bear you up, so that you will not dash your foot against a stone.'" Jesus said to him, "Again it is written, 'Do not put the Lord your God to the test.'" Again, the Devil took him to a very high mountain and showed him all the kingdoms of the world and their splendor; and he said to him, "All these I will give you, if you will fall down and worship me." Jesus said to him, "Away with you, Satan! for it is written, 'Worship the Lord your God, and serve only him.'" Then the Devil left him, and suddenly angels came and waited on him. (Matthew 4:1–11, *New Revised Standard Version*)

OCCUPYING TEMPTATION: WHO IS THE DEVIL?

Most people think of the Devil or Satan as the polar opposite of all that is godly and good. The figure of the Devil has been used throughout Christian history to personify the forces that oppose goodness in this world.

But isn't that exactly who the Devil or Satan is, the personification of all evil? Well, no, in truth. The Devil as he appears in the Hebrew Bible (what Christians call the Old Testament) is a servant of God. Satan means "obstructer or adversary" in Hebrew, and he is often sent by God as an adversary to human action. In Job, for example, God *sends* Satan to test Job by giving him many afflictions. It is the will of God that Satan do this, not Satan rebelling against the will of God.

Satan is also a figure used in the Hebrew Bible to describe the division and destruction within Israel. Satan is blamed for inciting dissension and discord among the people. In Isaiah, for example, Satan is personified as the "fallen angel," the servant of God who was insubordinate and fell from grace. *"How are you fallen from heaven, day star, son of dawn!"* (Isaiah 14:12) Satan, or Lucifer in Latin (meaning "light-bearer"), is the angel who wanted to be God and who was thrown out of heaven in disgrace. This figure causes a lot of trouble between God and humanity.

Elaine Pagels aptly summed up what the biblical figure of Satan really challenges us to confront: ". . . this greatest and most dangerous enemy did not originate, as one might expect, as an outsider, an alien, or a stranger. Satan is not the distant enemy but the intimate enemy—one's trusted colleague, close associate, brother . . . Whichever version of his origin one chooses, and there are many, all depict Satan as [an] *intimate* enemy—the attribute that qualifies him so well to express conflict among Jewish groups. Those who asked, 'How could God's own angel become his enemy?' were thus asking, in effect, 'How could one of *us* become one of *them*?'"[39]

This is, of course, also the question confronting the followers of Jesus who composed the Gospels. In their struggle within and with traditional Jewish teaching and practice of the time, these writers of the Gospels (composed between 70 and 100 C.E.), reformer Jews who were followers of Jesus of Nazareth, were trying to figure out why their own religious fellows rejected them, sometimes violently. Matthew shows Jesus in a titanic struggle with the Jewish religious leaders of his time, the Scribes and Pharisees, whom Jesus denounces as "child[ren] of hell" (Matt. 23:15). This struggle reaches its Gospel climax in John.

At the deepest level, the Devil and the seemingly cosmic struggle with evil he represents is always an incredibly intimate struggle. It is not the struggle with the enemy far off, but with the friend, the neighbor, and ultimately oneself. The Devil is not pure evil; he is the temptation within, the human struggle to be good in a very broken and conflicted world. The only way to really understand the Devil is to understand and come to terms with the very human temptation to abuse the power we have over one another.

EVEN THE DEVIL CAN OCCUPY SCRIPTURE

The phrase "even the Devil can quote scripture" comes from the biblical text in Matthew (and one in Luke 22) with which this chapter begins, where Jesus and the Devil are arguing, and they are *both quoting scripture* to make their case for and against giving in to temptation. Both Jesus and the Devil are, in effect, trying to occupy scripture here, in the sense that they're each trying to get some meaning from the text in the context of a life-and-death power struggle.

Biblical scholars have debated for centuries whether this text is a literal encounter between Jesus and the Devil or whether it is more of a parable, a story to teach about the reality of temptation—if even Jesus could be tempted, it's not surprising that human beings can be tempted as well.

Debates over events in the Bible and questions like, "did it really happen like that?" often distract people from the really crucial question about the Bible: "what does it actually mean for me, my life, and my society?" This is what I intend when I say the biblical text is talking about what's real. Temptation is very real; we face it every day. What does this biblical passage teach us about what is real in our lives when it comes to temptation and how to resist it?

That's why the question of location, location, location is so important as we talk about the reality of what Jesus said and did. We need to connect the text to the reality at the street level and the threat to people's very capacity to exist, to survive. Temptation is different at street level than it is on the eighth floor. But the teachings of Jesus are teachings for all; temptation and resistance to temptation hit you in different ways depending on your location.

Jesus is starving, having fasted in the wilderness for forty days. This beginning tells us something fundamental about temptation. For something to tempt you, you've really got to want it bad. For a smoker trying to quit, putting a pack of cigarettes in front of him or her is a huge temptation. For someone who has never smoked, like me, it's no temptation at all. But I love chocolate; an unattended chocolate bar is a huge temptation to me.

So the Devil, who is an expert in understanding and finding human weakness, first tempts the starving Jesus with food. Jesus turns to scripture, quoting Deuteronomy 8:3: *"One does not live by bread alone, but by every word that comes from the mouth of the Lord."*

This text from the Hebrew Bible, and Jesus' quotation of it in the Christian scriptures, is often used to justify poverty and interpreted to mean, "if you really have faith, you don't need food." That's not at all what this text means, nor what Jesus means when he quotes it.

On the one hand, theology really is a matter of the stomach, as Gustavo Gutierrez told the portly professor at the faculty reception. But on the other hand, having food in your stomach isn't all there is to life. Having food is essential to life, but so is living a decent human life, one that is dignified as befitting those created in the Image of God, the Word that came out of God's mouth and made human beings more than animals.

Human beings need food, but they also need beauty and a life that is more than toil, and they crave one as much as the other. Workers want both bread and roses, as the famous labor chant inscribed on a banner carried by young girls marching in parade of striking workers in 1912 at Lawrence Textile in Lawrence, Massachusetts, stated.[40]

> *As we come marching, marching, in the beauty of the day . . .*
> *Our life shall not be sweated from birth until life closes,*
> *Hearts starve as well as bodies, give us Bread but give us Roses!*

"Hearts starve as well as bodies, give us Bread but give us Roses!" has continued to mean labor struggles for wages and a decent human life, as the 2000 film by Ken Loach indicates. Closely based on the Justice for Janitors campaign undertaken in Los Angeles by the Service Employees International Union in 1990 that has spread to other cities, *Bread and Roses* is a fictionalized story of two Latinas in Los Angeles who struggle, along with a union organizer, to organize janitorial staff. Many of these janitors are women and immigrant, and the film links their struggles to the Lawrence strike.[41] These workers argue about job security and whether labor activism is too risky, but they also dance furiously and love passionately. They eat wonderful bread, but like Jesus, cannot live by bread alone. Human beings need more than bread, these Latina organizers contend. Jesus makes the same argument, so the Devil tries another tack.

The Devil tries to get Jesus "high" on power by taking him up to "the pinnacle of the temple, saying to him, 'If you are the Son of God, throw yourself down; for it is written, "He will command his angels concerning you," and "On their hands they will bear you up, so that you will not dash your foot against a stone."'"

If bread isn't tempting enough, the Devil seems to be saying, what about religious power? The temple in Jerusalem in Jesus' time was an incredible structure. When Jesus came to Jerusalem, the Temple had just been stunningly rebuilt by Herod the Great. The Temple area had been enlarged to a size of about 35 acres. The Jewish historian Josephus raved about the Temple, especially the use of white marble to give it a "natural magnificence."[42] The temple sat on the highest hill in Jerusalem.

Even though the Romans occupied Israel in Jesus' time, the religious authorities still wielded considerable power, as is clear in the biblical narratives about the accusation, arrest, and subsequent execution of Jesus. But the religious authorities had even more power over the religious lives of Jews, including Jesus. They are the ones who occupied the sacred texts, rendering judgments on the orthodoxy of the scripture that guided the lives of Jewish believers. In the Christian scriptures, Jesus is often found contending fiercely with Jewish leaders over the meaning of texts.

So in taking Jesus up to the top of the temple, the Devil knew to tempt him by offering to let him lord it over the religious authorities who were so opposed to his efforts and show them who's who! What a rush it would have been to go up to the very top of this magnificent symbol of Jewish tradition and authority and just dive off and have angels catch you. The Devil even quotes a Psalm, 91:12, to support his tempting offer! That would show those Jewish leaders who had dismissed Jesus as a naïve country preacher.

"Do not put the Lord your God to the test," Jesus replies, countering the Devil's use of a Psalm with Deuteronomy 6:16.

In the face of the Devil's temptations, Jesus consistently quotes Deuteronomy, and he quotes each time from the same part of that book. The full verse in Deuteronomy states, *"Do not put the Lord your God to the test, as you tested him at Massah."* What happened at Massah?

"Massah" actually means "test" in Hebrew, and Moses gave this name to the place where the Israelites, in the wilderness, grumble about not having enough water, testing God. It's not enough, apparently, that the tent-making God has been with them in the past; right now they are questioning whether God is still with their movement.

> *[The] whole congregation of the Israelites journeyed by stages, as the Lord commanded. They camped at Rephidim, but there was no water for the people to drink. The people quarreled with Moses, and said, "Give us water to drink." Moses said to them, "Why do you quarrel with me? Why do you test the Lord?" But the people thirsted there for water; and the people complained against Moses and said, "Why did you bring us out of Egypt, to kill us and our children and livestock with thirst?" So Moses cried out to the Lord, "What shall I do with this people? They are almost ready to stone me." The Lord said to Moses, "Go on ahead of the people, and take some of the elders of Israel with you; take in your hand the staff with which you struck the Nile, and go. I will be standing there in front of you on the rock at Horeb. Strike the rock, and water will come out of it, so that the people may drink." Moses did so, in the sight of the elders of Israel. He called the place Massah and Meribah, because the Israelites quarreled and tested the Lord, saying, "Is the Lord among us or not?"* (Exodus 17:1–7)

Israel had seen God do great things in the past. God had saved them from Egyptian slavery and parted the Red Sea, God had been with this movement. So where was God *now*?

In the Civil Rights movement, there were times when it was clear that God was with the movement. Andrew Young, then an aide to Dr. King, recalls a march in Birmingham, Alabama, after Dr. King had been arrested and put in jail. The marchers were heading for the jail when police with dogs and fire trucks abruptly stopped them. They were told, "You can't go any further." Young recalls that a woman cried out, "God is with this movement," and people fell down and moaned in prayer. Then they started singing, "I want Jesus to walk with me," and got up and continued the march. The police line parted, "the dogs fell silent," and another woman cried out, "Great God Almighty, he parted the Red Sea one more time."[43]

But where was God when Civil Rights demonstrators were beaten and set upon by dogs, fire hosed, arrested, and even murdered?

Christians are prone to assume that if Jesus had thrown himself down from the pinnacle of the Temple, giving in to the Devil's temptation, angels would have shown up. But in quoting Deuteronomy, and connecting the Devil's temptation to the testing of God in the wilderness, Jesus helps us to go deeper. For those involved with occupying the Bible in particular, we have to confront the fact that despite being a movement God, God does not always show up in the way we might want, exactly when we want. You can die in the wilderness. Maybe there will be water, and maybe there won't. It's possible that if you throw yourself off of the pinnacle of the Temple, the angels will show up—and maybe they won't.

High-pressure water stream from a fire hose pummels protestors in Birmingham, Alabama.
Corbis/Bettman Collection via Associated Press, 1963

It's possible the armed authorities will let you march, as in Birmingham, but sometimes, as happened in the anti-Vietnam War student protest at Kent State University, the National Guard opens fire and kills and injures people and we ask, "where is God in this?"

OVERREACHING: THE CORRUPTIONS OF POWER

Again, the Devil took him to a very high mountain and showed him all the kingdoms of the world and their splendor; and he said to him, "All these I will give you, if you will fall down and worship me."

So, failing twice to convince Jesus to give in to temptation, the Devil plays his trump card. Absolute political power. All the "glory" and "all this authority" of the kingdoms of the world belong to the Devil, and the Devil promises it all to Jesus if only Jesus will worship him.

What does it say about absolute political power that in the Bible this is the realm under the sway of Satan, and that Satan gives or withholds political power as he will?

The model for political power in the time of Jesus is Roman imperial power. Israel had been conquered by the dominant political power of the time, which was one of the most viciously ruthless in history. The Romans were a slave society that dominated much of the known world through the exercise of power backed up by brute force. The Roman military, without which Roman rule could not have survived, let alone been so extended, was justly famed for its discipline and its military tactics. It combined the practicality of engineering, such as road building, with a merciless, relentless mastery of military tactics. The Romans enslaved many of those they subjugated, and Roman society was built on a slave system. Slaves, often subject to brutal conditions, revolted several times, and the Roman response was military conquest and terror. After putting down the slave revolt led by the gladiator Spartacus, for example, the six thousand slaves not killed in battle were crucified along the Appian Way.

This is the model of authority that the Devil is using to tempt Jesus.

The Bible is showing us a model of political power as tyranny, and when we occupy this text, we see that tyrannical political power that enslaves and rules by force and the threat of force is what the biblical authors consider evil. This is the kind of power with which Satan tempts Jesus, the power of tyranny.

What is evil about tyrannical political power? It corrupts, and as Lord Acton reminds us, "absolute power corrupts absolutely."[44] The capacity to exercise unchecked power tempts us to abuse power, to overreach and subjugate others.

When University of California, Davis, Police Lieutenant John Pike casually pepper-sprayed nonviolent students seated in protest on their own campus, it was the lieutenant's relaxed posture combined with his brutal action that sparked particular outrage. The excessive use of force, the casual spraying of a toxic chemical directly into the faces of peacefully protesting students, became a symbol for the overreaching

Students at University of California, Davis, are casually pepper-sprayed by campus police lieutenant John Pike.
REUTERS/Brian Nguyen, November 18, 2011

of American political power in attempting to suppress the #Occupy movement.

Not only were peaceful protestors physically abused and harassed by an increasingly militarized police response to #Occupy, reporters trying to cover the mistreatment of #Occupy demonstrators were themselves beaten and arrested, and attempts were made to prevent them from actually reporting on this abuse of power. In early 2012, Reporters Without Borders released an updated "Press Freedom Index." The United States fell 27 places to 47th place, a fall as precipitous as that of Bahrain in the wake of the suppression of journalists in that repressive society. The report summary indicates that the huge decline in the press freedom ranking of the United States was due to the many arrests of journalists covering the #Occupy movement.[45]

When we occupy the biblical story of the temptation of Jesus by Satan, we have to do so in relationship to the struggle over religious power between the followers of Jesus of Nazareth and the religious establishment of his time and the increasingly repressive Roman military occupation of Israel. This whole story tells us a lot about the capacity of unchecked power to overreach, and that's where its weakness lies.

HOW JESUS DEFEATS THE DEVIL

> *Jesus said to him, "Away with you, Satan! for it is written, 'Worship the Lord your God, and serve only him.'"*

It is ironic that through this very overreaching of power, the Devil, and by extension, tyrannical power, is defeated. The early Christian theologians, living under Roman rule and horribly oppressed by the Roman Empire, understood this. Viewing the Bible from the street, they saw that evil, Satan among us, is unjust and violent abuse of power. Later Christians, who had a Holy Roman Empire of their own, moved into the equivalent of the eighth floor and abandoned the idea of evil as tyrannical and abusive power, instead seeing it as failure to obey the authority of the ruling religious and political elites.

But Irenaeus, a second century theologian, for example, understood that Satan "tyrannized over us unjustly."[46] God, in Irenaeus's view, does not respond violently to Satan's tyranny over God's children, humanity. Instead, God uses Satan's own weakness, the fact that those who crave absolute power will always want to get even more power and so they *overreach.*

What God does, according to Irenaeus, is use nonviolence as a way to lure the Devil into overreaching, going after the one sinless human being who doesn't deserve to die. God tricks Satan. When God became human, God "baffled His adversary" the Devil and "exhausted the force" of his attack.[47] The Devil's own moral bankruptcy is exposed, and human beings can see the Satanic abuse of power for what it really is and thus can escape being enslaved by it.

The #Occupy protests exhibit all the dynamics of the nonviolent direct action movements of the twentieth century as seen in the work of Mohandas K. Gandhi as well as Dr. King, and the April 6 movement in Egypt that so symbolized the Arab Spring with young Egyptians chanting "peaceful, peaceful."[48]

And as in Cairo and New York and Birmingham, they were met with force, sometimes even with brutality.

The police response follows Gandhi's prescription for why nonviolence is so effective: nonviolent protest exposes the underlying brutality of unjust systems and the dilemma that nonviolence poses to armed authority. The pepper spraying at UC Davis and other shocking acts of police brutality illustrate what Gandhi taught: "First they ignore you, then they laugh at you, then they fight you, then you win." And Gandhi's followers didn't even have cell phones that could film all of the violence that erupts when nonviolent direct action grows in numbers and support. A "UC Davis Protestors Peppered Sprayed" YouTube video showing Lt. Pike and colleagues in action had nearly 1.75 million views. An "NYPD pepper sprays peaceful protesters" YouTube video had over 1,300,000 views as of this writing.

Those at the top, the 1%, are tempted to abuse power to try to control the people. They overreach, and when they do, the demonic face of unjust power can be seen and even more clearly resisted.

Nonviolent direct action has been employed to great effect in the twentieth century because it exposes how power is actually distributed in a society. The people on the street are the ones who have the most power in a society; they need only realize it. Jesus of Nazareth knew this in the first century, and so did the early church until Christians became the ruling authorities and power infiltrated and corrupted them.

This is the lesson we need to learn today in answer to "what does this biblical text mean for me, my life, and my society?" The temptation to abuse power is not only seen in the use of force. Money is an enormous source of temptation; the desire for money is the hook the Devil uses to lure humanity into becoming ever more greedy.

3

Den of Thieves

An Occupy protestor in London dressed as Jesus.
Ilias Bartolini, October 15, 2011

Then Jesus entered the temple and drove out all who were selling and buying in the temple, and he overturned the tables of the money changers and the seats of those who sold doves. He said to them, "It is written, 'My house shall be called a house of prayer;' but you are making it a den of robbers." (Matthew 21:12–13, *New Revised Standard Version*)

DEN OF THIEVES

When Jesus drove the money changers out of the Temple in Jerusalem, he took on the brokers (bankers) ripping off the pilgrims who came during Passover. These brokers worked with the priestly class who ran the Temple, and together they had made the Temple in Jerusalem a powerful center of economic activity. These bankers would sell their own Temple coinage in exchange for foreign money but charge interest in the process, hence making it into a "den of robbers" or, as in older translations, a "den of thieves."

The Temple in Jerusalem was, of course, an important center of Jewish religious life. But it was also, in a sense, the national bank of Israel in Jesus' time because it was one of the most secure places in Israel to keep money.[49] Thus it became a powerful national treasury that did not let its great wealth sit idle. The Temple lent the money it collected and again charged interest, a practice that actually violated Jewish tradition, especially when the loans were made to the poor or within the Jewish community. Jesus was incensed at these Temple practices that drove the Jewish people into debt while serving the interests of the Jerusalem elites.

Yes, credit and debt are religious issues! Jesus plainly thought so, to the point where he physically disrupted the largest national bank in Israel during the height of its Passover practice of ripping off the poor and affluent pilgrims alike.

BIBLICAL BANKING

The whole issue of charging interest on loans and poor people falling further and further into debt is a huge biblical issue and one that, if we #OccupytheBible, we can see is very much at the center of Jesus' teaching and actions.

Three places in the Hebrew Bible show us what biblical banking is supposed to be. In all three places, charging interest to the poor, that is, driving them into debt, is forbidden as in Exodus 22:25–27, Leviticus 25:36–37, and Deuteronomy 23:20–21.

Clearly, in biblical times, lending money, especially to the poor, was a common practice. But Exodus warns the lender against treating the loan as a money-making transaction: "you shall not deal with them as a creditor; you shall not exact interest from them." Taking a pledge for security on the loan is okay, but when you lend to the poor, you need to take care that if you take "your neighbor's cloak in pawn, you shall restore it before the sun goes down, for it may be your neighbor's only clothing to use as cover; in which else shall that person sleep?" And you'd better pay attention, because if you treat lending to the poor as a money-making business, and the poor cry out to God, "I will listen, for I am compassionate."

In short, it's acceptable to lend to the poor, but don't treat it as a business from which you are going to make a lot of money, don't charge interest, and be compassionate about how you handle their security on the loan.

In Leviticus, loans themselves are encouraged, whether of money or food, but just as in Exodus, money lent to the poor should not be at interest, and food sold to the poor should not be at a profit. In Deuteronomy, it's okay to charge a foreigner interest, but not a fellow Jew. Taking someone's means of livelihood (i.e., a millstone used to grind corn) as security for a loan is also forbidden.

But by the time of Jesus, some Jews had apparently begun to disregard these sacred Jewish teachings on how to lend money without driving people into poverty. How people paid the "Temple tax" is one important example of how these rules about interest and lending were being bent and even broken.

Especially at Passover, Jerusalem teemed with Jews. The Jewish historian Josephus says they were "an innumerable multitude"[50] and each had come to pay money to the Temple. Every Israelite male over twenty, rich or poor, was required to pay half a shekel to the Temple treasury as an offering. No "foreign money" was allowed, which is why the money changers Jesus threw out of the Temple were changing the pilgrims' money from their local coinage to shekels, as we noted in the beginning of this chapter.

The money changers, according to Jesus, were robbing people by doing this. A trip to the Temple was expensive. Not only could exchanging money be expensive, there was also the cost of animal sacrifice. Remember, Jesus drove out not just the money changers, but also "those who sold doves," typically the sacrificial animal the poor could afford.[51]

Jesus wasn't surprised to find commerce going on in the Temple. After all, it's not surprising to go into a bank and find banking going on. This commercial activity was normal in Jerusalem. What Jesus objected to was what this economic activity had become—ruling-class interests dominating Temple activity—and it's these "Temple entrepreneurs"[52] Jesus attacked.

Tremendous wealth had accumulated in Jerusalem because of all of the money the Temple collected, and it wasn't sitting idle. It was lent out with interest, and these practices drove the large number of poor in the city even further into debt. The Romans and their tax system also contributed to the gap between Jerusalem's 1% and 99% in Jesus' time. Tax gatherers, who are so clearly hated in the Gospel accounts, could make themselves rich through fraud. Some of them not only had huge homes in Jerusalem, but also country estates. The vast wealth of the 1% in Israel reached unbelievable proportions in the days of Herod.

This kind of #OccupytheBible analysis sheds new light on why Jesus went to Jerusalem during Passover. Did he go specifically to confront the unjust banking practices of his time? Did he go primarily to occupy a bank?

JESUS GOES TO WALL STREET: #OWS AND THE ECONOMIC MELTDOWN OF 2008

Out-of-control banking practices were, without a doubt, a significant factor in creating the economic crisis in 2008 in the United States. This is not the only cause of the gross economic inequality that has developed in America, which has been 30 years in the making. The CBO chart reproduced on page 4 makes that clear.

But the near-term reason the U.S. banking industry could well be described as a "den of thieves" like the Temple treasury of Jesus' time starts with what are called sub-prime mortgages. These mortgages have artificially low interest rates and are given to high-risk borrowers who put little or no money down. The sting in the tail is that these mortgages cruelly targeted those who wanted to buy a home but were financially not in a position to do so. And when the housing market collapsed, these were the people in the economy least able to stay current on their loans, as many lost their jobs. Or, if they kept their jobs, they still found they were "upside down" on their loans, as their houses were worth far less than the value of the loan itself.[53]

To add to the banking industry's irresponsible behavior in causing the economic meltdown that began in earnest in 2007, these bad mortgages were bundled up and sold as investments to others, thus divesting the lenders of any responsibility for the loan and any worries about whether they would or could be paid back. The bundles of bad loans were often given great ratings by risk insurers because those evaluating the risk had become part of the banking industry.[54]

Paul Krugman, the Nobel Prize–winning economist and harsh critic of these practices, said "buying these derivatives [which brought down the banks] was like buying insurance for the Titanic from someone on the Titanic." The whole mess, according to Krugman, is a regulatory failure. "A 'shadow banking system' developed where more and more of the world's transactions were conducted by institutions that were not subject to traditional banking regulation."[55]

If you watch FOX News you might think that #Occupy-WallStreet is a giant socialist proto-revolution, or a bunch of crazy people, or both.[56] But the goals of #OWS are very focused on how deregulation of the banking industry is a primary cause of the explosion of economic inequality in this country. That is why #OWS protestors were holding signs calling for the reinstatement of the Glass-Steagall Act[57] in November 2011.[58]

#OccupytheSEC (Securities and Exchange Commission) was even more specific on what needs to happen to rein in the risky financial practices that contribute to such gross economic inequality in the United States. This Occupy group held a march to deliver a 325-page letter to the SEC calling for it to strengthen—and then, more important, enforce—the Volcker Rule, which went into effect on July 21, 2012. The purpose of the Volker Rule is to curb risky speculative trading by Wall Street investment firms. As well-paid lobbyists do their best to create loopholes through which the banks can crawl to continue their dangerous, unregulated activity, this group of Occupiers is pushing for stronger regulation and enforcement.[59]

DEVIL IN A PIN-STRIPED SUIT

So is the banking industry the new face of Satan in this country?

The Devil can certainly be portrayed as a lawyer. He was personified this way in Hollywood films such as *The Devil's Advocate*, where Al Pacino, as Satan, is a senior partner in a law firm. Satan tempts the aspiring young lawyer Keanu Reeves into selling his soul to be able to "win at any cost."[60]

But Hollywood has also portrayed bankers as the root of all evil—well, bankers and those in related financial industries. Just ask Oliver Stone,[61] whose movie *Wall Street* features the classic Satanic Wall Street character Gordon Gecko, played by Michael Douglas, who declares passionately to an audience of stunned shareholders of a small paper mill:

> *"Greed, for lack of a better word, is good. Greed is right, greed works. Greed clarifies, cuts through, and captures the essence of the evolutionary spirit. Greed, in all of its forms; greed for life, for money, for love, knowledge has marked the upward surge of mankind. And greed, you*

mark my words, will not only save Teldar Paper, but that other malfunctioning corporation called the USA."

As we discussed in Chapter 2, the Devil is not an external enemy, but an intimate enemy. The Devil is temptation within, the human struggle to be good in a broken and conflicted world. The only way to really understand the Devil is to understand yourself and your own capacity to fall into temptation.

We've all got to do a lot more soul-searching to figure out how, as a nation, we came to accept that living on credit was a good thing. Many people decided it was just fine to build an economy that was focused not on producing jobs, but on creating and selling debt to the unsuspecting. *Hey, as long as the price of my house goes up, why should I care?*

Well, we should have cared because more and more fellow Americans were out of work or have had their salaries reduced and their benefits cut, and millions upon millions don't have health insurance. And if you were one of the people who didn't benefit from the booming debt economy, your cries fell on deaf ears.

Ask yourself this, too, as long as we're engaging in an honest look into what the Devil and temptation really mean: when GOP presidential candidate Mitt Romney, a very wealthy man, said that the criticism of his low tax rate was motivated by envy, couldn't there have been a grain of truth in that? Might we, just ever so slightly, wish we were he?[62]

We all played a role in creating the conditions where an economy that didn't make anything but debt and hardly produced any jobs was regarded as a good thing. It's true that some people are more to blame than others for their direct role in creating the financial instruments that got us to this pass, or for failing to regulate them when they were so clearly risky. But screwing up the economy by deregulation and excessive lending took a long time. People have been losing good jobs and losing their healthcare and other benefits for decades now. Where was the outcry when the market was at 14,000?

As the Bible and history show us, the practice of exploiting the poor and the middle class is not new. What *is* new, however, is that we have abandoned everything we learned in this country about how to control the worst of these banking abuses. In the mid-twentieth century we figured out that the markets—and the banks—needed to be regulated, and we introduced rules to oversee lending practices and rein in at least the worst of the sinful human impulse toward greed and exploitation.

The Great Depression of the 1930s was in part a result of Herbert Hoover's overconfidence that business would regulate itself. After the Crash of 1929 and the Depression that followed, regulations were put in place to restrain the most extreme and riskiest practices of financial markets.

These regulations stayed in place until the Reagan Revolution of the 1980s, and the tide of free market economics that followed has nearly destroyed the American economy. Deregulating the banking industry has allowed it to rip off the poor and the middle class and provide more profit to wealthy elites who are currently (in 2012) pouring money into an electoral system that has given them permission, via the Supreme Court's Citizen's United ruling, to maintain their power by outspending any opposition three or four to one, in some cases.[63]

It takes enablers of the economic system to do this; it takes those who can interpret economic systems to justify that free markets will create a rising tide for everybody. Today these are the think tanks such as the Hoover Institute or the American Enterprise Institute, and those who follow the theories of economics professor Milton Friedman, called a "market fundamentalist" for his unwavering ideology that markets always get it right and regulation only gets in the way of capitalist productivity.

In Jesus' time, it was the Scribes he went after for providing the legal reasons the banking practices that harmed the poor were just fine.

After Jesus drives the money changers out of the Temple, he stays in Jerusalem, teaching the people. Jesus' teaching matches his actions in occupying the biggest bank in Jerusalem. He teaches about how the religious elites in Jerusalem are robbing the poor, such as widows. Jesus warns his disciples in front of "all the people" so everybody hears it (and we can assume his warning would quickly get back to those religious elites) that ripping off the poor through tricky legal maneuvers has got to stop. He warns his disciples of the condemnation that is coming for the Scribes.

Scribes in Jesus' time were not just those who wrote. They were a special group among the Jewish religious leaders. They were supposed to study the Law of Moses, teach it to the people, and inform on questions of law. This gave them a lot of power. Too much power, Jesus seemed to think, which had gone to their heads. Jesus tells everybody that the Scribes like to show off in the marketplaces with their long robes and take the best seats at the synagogues and banquets. But "they devour widows' houses."

The Scribes are stealing these widows' houses? How? If the banking practices of the Temple were anything to go by, perhaps by their interpretation of the banking regulations. According to Jesus, the Scribes' interpretation of the law plainly wasn't a good deal for poor widows. (Luke 20:45–47)

In the spring of 2012, the #Occupy movement started to work on stopping foreclosures and keeping people in their homes. #Occupy helped 83-year-old Mercedes Robinson-Duvallon, an elderly wheelchair-bound woman in Miami, whom sheriff's deputies tried to evict.[64] A national group, occupyyourhomes.org, shows that "more than 100 groups" have formed to work on foreclosures.

We need to #Occupy the actions and teachings of Jesus on unfair banking practices and the way they prey upon the poor and the vulnerable. This is a lesson for all of us, not just the 1%. And we need to go after the think tank enablers of banking deregulation and risky investment practices, not just the practitioners.

To challenge the systems that are creating such wealth for the 1% and such poverty and lack of opportunity for the 99%, it is crucial to organize. That is why the history of workers getting together to organize is such an important lesson for how we move forward. It is startling to realize that Jesus also thought labor organizing could help build a movement that really understands what's happening to ordinary people.

4

Did Jesus Organize a Union?

As Jesus passed along the Sea of Galilee, he saw Simon and his brother Andrew casting a net into a lake—for they were fishermen. And Jesus said to them, "Follow me and I will make you fish for people." And immediately they left their nets and followed him. As he went a little farther, he saw James son of Zebedee and his brother John, who were mending the nets. Immediately he called them; and they left their father Zebedee in the boat with the hired men, and followed him. (Mark 1:16–20, *New Revised Standard Version*)

When Jesus wants to start his ministry, he walks all the way to the Galilee from his home in Nazareth to recruit followers. Why not just recruit followers from among the people he knew in his hometown? And why specifically recruit fishermen?

John Dominic Crossan, in his book *God and Empire: Jesus Against Rome Then and Now,*[65] offers an answer to these questions. Crossan points out that the Roman imperial project of commercializing the fishing industry took place during the time of Jesus. Herod Antipas, the provincial Roman governor, was regulating and taxing the indigenous fishing industry around the Sea of Galilee pretty much out of profitability.

The occasion for Crossan's reflection on what was happening to the formerly prosperous fishing villages is the discovery of a sunken fishing vessel, probably from between 100 BCE and 67 CE. This vessel was discovered during a drought that shrunk the Sea of Galilee and exposed the wreck. What remained of the fishing boat had been patched and patched and patched with different kinds of wood until it had been stripped of every useful piece and the rest pushed out to sea, providing insight into what happened to the fishers under Roman rule. The boat shows how they fell on hard times and "had to nurse their boats for as long as possible."[66] These formerly prosperous fishing families were now scraping to keep their boats and their lives together under the ruinous economic practices of Imperial Rome.

Crossan argues that Jesus wanted to call disciples who would understand the stark difference between his teaching that "the kingdom of God is in your midst" and the kingdom of Caesar being forced on the Jews by imperial Rome. Antipas began to "commercialize the lake [Sea of Galilee] and its fishers in the name of Rome's empire and both John and Jesus clashed with him in the name of Israel's God."

Another factor that is relevant to this text is the history of Roman military occupation of Israel. After the death of Herod the Great in 4 CE, Jewish revolts broke out all over. According to Josephus in his *Jewish War*, the town of Sepphoris, not four miles from Nazareth, was a center of the rebellion and the recipient of the worst Roman military suppression of the revolt. The city was captured and burned, and its inhabitants enslaved.[67] This violent clampdown on Jewish resistance took place around the time Jesus was born. Jesus would surely have grown up hearing about the violence of Roman rule and what happens to those who challenge Roman authority directly.

Thirty years after the death of Jesus, it happened again. Another Jewish rebellion broke out against the Roman occupation. This became a horrible and devastating war, culminating in massacre and the destruction of the Temple in Jerusalem by the Roman legions. All the Gospels were composed after the destruction of the temple, the Gospel of Mark almost immediately in the wake of that devastating event, possibly even during it, and the others somewhat later. In this sense, all that we know of Jesus, his life, his teachings, and his death and resurrection should be read as wartime literature—and understood in that light.

The Jewish community was divided during this long and devastating war. Jewish soldiers put down the rebellion and massacre of their own, the Temple elite sold out their fellow Jews in order to continue their own power, and people from the countryside openly and violently rebelled against Rome. As with all conflict in repressive situations, the cycle of violence is positively demonic in intensity. This is certainly true not only after the death of Jesus, but also during Jesus' time, and certainly in Jesus' view.

All the Gospels record that one day, after Jesus had established his ministry in Galilee, he crossed the Sea of Galilee and encountered a wild man who was possessed by demons, by the Devil. When Jesus speaks to the demons he asks, "What is your name?" They said, "Legion" for as the text says, "we are many." (Mark 5:9; Luke 8:30)

But what is a legion? A legion can certainly mean "a lot of demons" but *legion* is more commonly the term for the heavy infantry that was the basic military unit of the ancient Roman army during the empire. It was a division of a couple thousand Roman soldiers, though the number could vary. It almost always had attached to it one or more units of conscripted troops (i.e., non-Roman citizens). In Jesus' time, these conscripts would have been Jews.

The demons, or more likely the oppressive legions of Romans and their Jewish auxiliary, are "called out" by Jesus, and *two thousand of them* rush into a herd of swine and are drowned. In ancient Israel, the eating of pork was forbidden, so being called a swine was not a compliment, even as in most cultures today it is not a term of praise. These demons, as we used to say of authority figures in the sixties, are the pigs, and it is interesting that their number of two thousand approximates a Roman Legion.

The Gospels need to be read through movement eyes, through the lives of people who are struggling economically and whose lives, property, and businesses are being dominated by an unjust system. Read as wartime literature, these texts have to be examined through the lens of an occupied people whose most intimate enemy was themselves, the hated Jewish troops, the Temple elite, and even the violent subversives whose rebellion provoked the worst of all destructions: that of the temple.

When Jesus went to the Sea of Galilee to start his ministry, he was not just calling individual disciples. He was starting a movement among those who would see the difference between the rule of the divine Caesar under the repression of the Roman occupiers and their Jewish collaborators, and what Jesus called the Kingdom of God.

In the movement building that was Jesus' ministry, labor justice is part of the program; thus Jesus did organize labor. But organizing among those who worked and who were suffering under the economic practices of the time was not an end in itself. Jesus' broader program included healing, eating and drinking with friends and with those who have been excluded, and enacting a new understanding of community based on mutuality and peace, not violence and greed.

Jesus organized workers into his disciples because they were the people who understood the difference between work as exploitation in the service of greed and work as a means to feed their families and benefit their communities.

This threatened Roman rule and the consolidation of imperial economic power backed up by military power. It's no surprise, therefore, that Jesus' efforts to bring in a new reign of justice for workers was met with violence.

This has often been true of the American labor movement as well.

UNIONIZATION AND THE KINGDOM OF GOD

Jesus sends the disciples out to labor and tells them to accept food and housing because the "laborer deserves to be paid" (Luke 10:7). In the United States, labor unions developed in the nineteenth century as organizations of employees who banded together because they were not being paid decent wages and were forced to work in unsafe conditions for long hours.

Just over one hundred years ago, one of the worst industrial disasters in U.S. history took place—a fire in a substandard garment factory in New York City killed 146 workers,

Tragic casualties from the Triangle Shirtwaist factory fire.

Brown Brothers, March 25, 1911

Striking members of the International Ladies Garment Workers.

The Everett Collection, 1909

primarily women and girls. This is known as the Triangle Shirtwaist factory fire.[68]

The fire led to labor agitation and to the formation of the International Ladies Garment Workers Union (ILGWU), which fought for better working conditions for workers in that industry.

This is my family history, as my Hungarian ancestors worked as children and teenagers in the sweatshops of the garment district in New York City, and my Great Aunt Helen became a labor organizer for the ILGWU. Working conditions in many industries were terrible in that period of rapid industrialization. Children, women, and men worked in poor light, in freezing cold and broiling heat, for long hours without breaks and being paid less than a living wage. They organized, and with others in the labor movement they fought for and won the eight-hour day, an end to child labor, and forced their employers to improve safety and working conditions.

The Social Gospel movement was instrumental in these labor struggles. Indeed, this time in American religious history demonstrates that Christians in America have occupied the Bible before.

The Social Gospel was the effort of Christians in the late nineteenth and early twentieth century to shine the light of the Christian Gospel onto the appalling working conditions that had become commonplace in the rapid industrialization of that century. The Social Gospel, as exemplified in the work of Walter Rauschenbusch and Washington Gladden, took a new look at scripture from the perspective of these and other rampant social abuses.

One of the best-known works from this era, *Christianity and the Social Crisis*, was written by Rauschenbusch to bring "new social insight into the Gospel," and it is both original in its thought and highly relevant for the twentieth century. Rauschenbusch contends that unlike the men of "ripe age" who comment on the scriptures and pass on what they have been taught they should see there, those engaged with the current social crisis of the day would come to know Jesus in a new way, and, when they did, "the more social do his [Jesus'] thoughts and aims become."[69]

The purpose of Jesus' preaching is revealed, according to this social insight, as being in line with the prophets. Jesus preached the "Kingdom of God." Scholars disagree, Rauschenbusch observes, on whether this kingdom will be only in the future after the end of history, or whether it's supposed to be a "present reality." Well, while "others were scanning the horizon with a telescope to see it [the Kingdom of God] come; he [Jesus] said, 'It is already here, right in the midst of you.'" (Luke 17:21) The "future tense" changing to the "present tense" is the way Rauschenbusch and others in the Social Gospel movement occupied the Bible in light of the social crises of their day. Jesus couldn't wait, and neither, they argued, should Christians today.[70]

This leads to the ethical program of Jesus that, according to Rauschenbusch, is a social, not just an individual, ethics. "All human goodness must be social goodness," he wrote in the early twentieth century, as the social crisis around him woke him and others up to the core message of the New Testament. Being good as an individual was not sufficient; we needed to strive, thought Rauschenbusch, to be a good society.

The book was, by any measure, a bestseller. It was released in 1907 and for the next three years outsold any religious book except the Bible. It sold 50,000 copies in its first few printings.

But Social Gospel reformers like Rauschenbusch and Gladden were up against powerful forces that saw labor reform as a threat. Just like in the time of Jesus, labor movements were met with repression and sometimes even violence.

The Social Gospel was important to bring the Bible and Christian ethics to labor reform.

THE LEGIONS FIGHT BACK AGAINST LABOR REFORM

One of the worst instances of violence and then miscarriage of justice happened at Haymarket in Chicago in 1886 and is still remembered with a sculpture and commemorative activities. That year, a coalition of unionists, reformers, socialists, anarchists, and workers attempted to make Chicago the center of the struggle for the eight-hour workday. In early May, two striking workers at a McCormick Reaper plant had been killed when police fired into the crowd. Anarchists hastily called a meeting at the West Randolph Street Haymarket. The crowd was peaceful, the mayor in attendance. Then, as the crowd dwindled, police ordered people to disperse and a bomb was thrown at the police. Many were injured and eight ultimately died.

City leaders, both political and business, reacted by suppressing organizing and attacking "foreign-born influences." The bomb thrower was never identified, though hundreds were arrested. Ultimately, eight prominent anarchists, including speakers and writers, were tried, though there was no evidence they had anything to do with the bomb. Seven of the eight were sentenced to death. Legal appeals failed, and ultimately four were hanged, one committed suicide, and the others had their sentences commuted for lack of evidence.[71]

Chicago religious leaders did not protest this judicially organized violent backlash against worker organizations. Indeed, the media successfully painted the Haymarket bombing as a socialist/anarchist plot, and the resulting backlash helped destroy the Knights of Labor, America's largest and most inclusive labor organization of the time.[72] Labor unions were labeled a secularist threat.

In context, therefore, the insights of the Social Gospel in occupying scripture on behalf of labor reform becomes even more significant. These Social Gospel leaders and their writings and teachings became widely influential in bringing a religious basis to the reform movements that attacked many of these social issues, including child labor, the forty-hour work week, and the minimum wage. FDR's New Deal drew on the Social Gospel, as did Lyndon Johnson's concept of the Great Society and, above all, the Civil Rights movement. Dr. King wrote, "In the early '50s I read Walter Rauschenbusch's *Christianity and the Social Crisis*, a book which left an indelible impression on my thinking."[73]

Labor reform was a hallmark of the Civil Rights movement. No moment illustrates that better, or more accurately shows the forces of the "legions" pushing back violently against the rights of workers, than what happened in 1968.

THE MEMPHIS GARBAGE STRIKE

In 1968, Memphis garbage workers went on strike[74] over a long history of poor working conditions for these city workers and indifference to their situation. In February of that year, two Memphis garbage collectors, Echol Cole and Robert Walker, had been crushed to death by a malfunctioning truck.

Striking workers from the Memphis Department of Public Works.
© *Corbis, February 1968*

But when 1,300 African American men from the Memphis Department of Public Works went on strike, it was their basic human dignity that united them in protest.

These workers carried signs that read, "I am a Man." The strike, as is the case in the labor movement in general, was over basic human dignity and worth, not simply specific working conditions. The signs implied, "it's not right to do this to me, to us, because we are as fully human as you."

Local clergy members and community leaders took an active role in the campaign, which included boycotts and civil disobedience. Civil Rights leaders Roy Wilkins, James Lawson, Bayard Rustin, Ralph Abernathy, and Jesse Jackson, among others, participated during the course of the strike. Dr. King also took an active role.

But the strike was met, as strikes so often are, with a highly militarized response. As the photo shows, unarmed, peacefully marching protestors walked past heavily armed National Guardsmen.

Dr. King spoke to these workers the night before he was assassinated. The text of that famous speech is almost always reduced to King seeming to predict his own death. But he also says he is glad, glad that he has lived to see this age where God is in the struggle to establish justice on earth for workers:

> *And I see God working in this period of the twentieth century in a way that men, in some strange way, are responding—something is happening in our world. The masses of people are rising up. And wherever they are assembled today, whether they are in Johannesburg, South Africa; Nairobi, Kenya; Accra, Ghana; New York City; Atlanta, Georgia; Jackson, Mississippi; or Memphis, Tennessee—the cry is always the same—"We want to be free."*[75]

This is a labor struggle, says King, that is about more than labor. It's about dignity and being full human beings in God's world. "We are determined to be people. We are saying that we are God's children. And that we don't have to live like we are forced to live."[76]

And Dr. King, as he always did, occupied the Bible. This is the same struggle we see in the Bible, says King, from Amos to Jesus. And any preacher who speaks to the workers' struggle for decent wages, safe working conditions, and a forty-hour week must say those biblical words. "Somehow the preacher must be an Amos, and say, 'Let justice roll down like waters and righteousness like a mighty stream.' Somehow, the preacher must say with Jesus, 'The spirit of the Lord is upon me, because he hath anointed me to deal with the problems of the poor.'"[77]

The next day, Dr. King was shot and killed.

After Dr. King's assassination, negotiators in Memphis reached a deal on the right of the sanitation workers to organize and on their demands. Several months later, however, the union had to threaten another strike to get the city council to honor the deal.

The violence of the biblical legions acting out against Jesus' vision of the Kingdom of God is sickeningly characteristic of the response to the organization of workers, and it is certainly evident in the killing of Dr. King.

LABOR ORGANIZING AND THE KINGDOM OF GOD

Jesus was right. The Kingdom of God is now. In fact, the kingdom of God is among you. Nothing is more central to the immediacy of this claim than the rights of workers to join together and bargain collectively for better wages and working conditions.

Worker justice is not just a civil right, it is a fundamental acknowledgment that human beings have an inherent dignity and worth. This idea, that human dignity, what Christians call "the image of God," is the connection between Christian moral reasoning and action for worker rights in the Gospels, the Social Gospel, the Civil Rights movement, the Solidarity movement in Poland as seen in the work of John Paul II, and now in the #Occupy movement.

What makes us not only people, but human beings with dignity and transcendent worth, is our capacity to work creatively in this world. When a society exploits our contribution to the whole and refuses to recognize the moral obligation we have to one another to ensure decent working conditions, a living wage, and the means to support our families, it violates our human dignity and denies the reality of the Kingdom of God in our midst.

John Paul II, in his famous encyclical *On Human Work*, stated his deep conviction of the centrality of work to human dignity and our being created in the image of God. Work is fundamental to the truth of the human condition. Through work, Pope John Paul II argues, people become who they are intended to be. Through work, human beings share "in the activity of the Creator." Human dignity, therefore, should be regarded not as passive, but as active. Human potential is more fulfilled when people have the means to express their creativity, and an important way they do that is through work.

Paid labor, of course, is clearly not the only way human dignity is expressed. But when working conditions for employees are unsafe, wages are suppressed, benefits are denied or slashed, and people are refused the right even to act together to improve their work life through collective bargaining, something fundamental in the dignity of human beings is also denied.[78]

We need a new American populism that will fight for the rights of workers in this country as they are threatened yet again. This connection between work and human dignity is at the core of a moral vision to guide and shape a new Social Gospel based on the Gospel of Jesus Christ. From Jesus, to the Social Gospel, to Dr. Martin Luther King, Jr., and the Civil Rights movement, to labor struggles today, we have to recognize that if a society makes some of its members into "nobodies," that society is violating core moral values about how we should treat one another who, in the Christian faith, are called the Kingdom of God.

This is also our heritage as Americans—ordinary workers struggled and died for decent labor conditions to make this country into a place of opportunity. This is the American Dream, a moral vision of what it means to treat one another with decency.[79]

5

Parables, or Why Jesus Was Not a Free-Market Capitalist

"For it is as if a man, going on a journey, summoned his slaves and entrusted his property to them; to one he gave five talents, to another two, to another one, to each according to his ability. Then he went away. The one who had received the five talents went off at once and traded with them and made five more talents. In the same way, the one who had the two talents made two more talents. But the one who had received the one talent went off and dug a hole in the ground and hid his master's money. After a long time the master of those slaves came and settled accounts with them. Then the one who had received the five talents came forward, bringing five more talents, saying, 'Master, you handed over to me five talents; see, I have made five more talents.' His master said to him, 'Well done, good and trustworthy slave; you have been trustworthy in a few things, I will put you in charge of many things; enter into the joy of your master.' And the

one with two talents also came forward, saying 'Master, you handed over to me two talents; see, I have made two more talents.' His master said to him, 'Well done, good and trustworthy slave; you have been trustworthy in a few things, I will put you in charge of many things; enter into the joy of your master.' Then the one who had received the one talent also came forward, saying, 'Master, I knew that you were a harsh man, reaping where you did not sow, and gathering where you did not scatter seed; so I was afraid, and I went and hid your talent in the ground. Here you have what is yours.' But his master replied, 'You wicked and lazy slave! You knew, did you, that I reap where I did not sow, and gather where I did not scatter? Then you ought to have invested my money with the bankers, and on my return I would have received what was my own with interest. So take the talent from him and give it to the one with the ten talents. For to all those who have, more will be given, and they will have an abundance; but from those who have nothing, even what they have will be taken away. As for this worthless slave, throw him into the outer darkness, where there will be weeping and gnashing of teeth.'" (Matthew 25:14–30, *New Revised Standard Version*)

JESUS WAS NOT A FREE-MARKET CAPITALIST

The term *capitalist* appears nowhere in the Bible, of course; it is an invention of the modern industrial period. Free-market capitalism is an economic theory that holds that government regulation is not necessary or wise for capitalist systems. According to this view, the market works best when rational economic actors are allowed to act individually without the interference of regulations.[80]

But over and over again, both in Jesus' time and in the modern, industrial, and post-industrial periods, unchecked economic power has consolidated wealth in the hands of a few and created poverty for many. In fact, history shows that capitalism is most productive for whole societies when it is properly regulated, as the period of enormous American prosperity that followed from the regulations put in place after the Great Depression shows.

Today, as in Jesus' time, the drive to accumulate wealth is strong, however, and people often try to use scripture to justify the few having enormous wealth and the majority being driven into poverty.

The Parable of the Talents is a favorite of religious and political Christian conservatives, as it seems to them that Jesus was teaching folks how to invest capital to make more money. Tony Perkins of the Family Research Council interprets Luke's version of this parable just that way, arguing that "Jesus was a free marketer, not an Occupier."[81]

Perkins has to move the meaning of the parable into the future for it to support his anti-Occupy message. "As Jesus was about to enter Jerusalem for the last time, just before his crucifixion, he was keenly aware that his disciples greatly desired and even anticipated that the kingdom of God was going to be established immediately on the earth."[82] So in Perkins's interpretation, this teaching, which is apparently about saving for a rainy day, is really a way to break the news that the Kingdom is not about to happen now. In my view, what Perkins thinks Jesus is teaching is that you'd better look into a kind of spiritual 401(k) if you want to make it in the Kingdom of God.

Perkins and the free-market Christians want to take the Parable of the Talents out of day-to-day conflicts about money and power and spiritualize it to make it work in heaven. But, paradoxically, Perkins also seems to want the parable to work as a good investment strategy in the here and now. It's a kind of having your eschatological cake and eating it too, that is, wanting the Bible to be all about the great reward you'll get in heaven after you die, so don't try to make the economic system just here and now. But there's occasionally some slippage, and the message seems to be that the righteous can make good money here on earth.

After all, according to Perkins, the fact that "Jesus chose the free market system as the basis for this parable should not be overlooked."[83] And just in case you missed the point, in the free-market system, according to Perkins, there are winners and there are losers. Thus, in his view, the master is really a stand-in for Jesus, who wants us all to put as much money as possible in our spiritual 401(k)s, and also, apparently, in our earthly 401(k)s.

That's how the Parable of the Talents works for the community of the Family Research Council, with its Plutochratic [government by the wealthy], pro-business perspective, clearly more akin to the eighth floor of the Chicago Mercantile Exchange view. They're either the 1% themselves, or they're supporting the practices of the 1%.

As I've said, it's location, location, location when it comes to the Bible, not only in the twenty-first century, but in the first century as well. The locations of the communities that give rise to the Gospels of Luke and Matthew cause them to interpret the parable in light of their concerns, which were about the future and what to do until Jesus returned. These communities were hugely concerned about the delay in Jesus' return and about the social and political crises each community faced because of conflicts with Rome and with the Jewish authorities who did not consider Jesus the Messiah. As with all of the Gospels, as was noted earlier, these texts are constructed for the instruction of communities grappling with the crises of their time and trying to understand Jesus' teaching in light of that.

But Jesus had a community, too. Jesus taught his followers to help them understand what the Kingdom of God looked like in their midst and how that contrasted with the Roman imperial rule and the role of the Temple elites.

What can we discern of what Jesus taught from the particular theologies of those Gospels? One immediately apparent conclusion we can draw is that this parable is really about the evils of excessive interest, as I wrote in Chapter 3. In Jewish history, gaining a lot of interest on an investment is something that the prophets teach over and over again should not be done, or should be done only within strict guidelines to prevent usury—the gouging and exploitation of the poor.

And what are we to make of the master, who is "harsh" and who "reaps where he does not sow"? Is he Jesus, or is he a wealthy man who gets even wealthier by violating Jewish law and investing with the bankers who were ripping off the poor at the Temple in Jerusalem? When the master rails at the third slave for just burying the money, he screams at him precisely for not investing with the bankers.

> *You knew, did you, that I reap where I did not sow, and gather where I did not scatter? Then you ought to have invested my money with the bankers, and on my return I would have received what was my own with interest.*

The Parable of the Talents is a "Text of Terror." This phrase was coined by Phyllis Trible, a feminist New Testament theologian, who published an important work on biblical texts about violence against women called *Texts of Terror*.[84]

Richard Lohrbaugh borrowed the Trible theme of terror to develop a street-level reading of the Parable of the Talents that shows it to be a tale of fear and loathing of the very rich who were breaking with tradition and trying to multiply their great wealth unjustly.[85] In contrast to the capitalist West, where making a lot of money through industrious investing is considered a good thing, traditional, agrarian societies do not believe this is a positive value, and it is certainly not positive according to the teachings of traditional Judaism on making money through investing, as was noted in Chapter 3.

Jesus taught in an agrarian society mostly made up of poor peasants and a servant/artisan class, with a very few elites who controlled most of the wealth. As a carpenter, Jesus came from the artisan class, so he knew the lives of the wealthier class and the lives of the poor who made up the majority of the society. Jesus knew the lives of those who worked the fields or tended animals, or who were slaves or servants of the rich, as is clear from the daily lives that form the locations of so many of the parables.

The main teaching of Jesus' ministry was that the "Kingdom of God is among you" (Luke 17:21). Jesus went to great lengths to contrast the present reality of God's kingdom with the present reality of the kingdom of the Roman armies occupying Israel, with the cooperation of the Temple elites. With all that in mind, then, we should realize that the Parable of the Talents must somehow be about resolving those two contrasting realities.

In Jesus' time, there was an increasingly wealthy urban class that had benefited by the redistribution of wealth upward through lending that increased debt, and from the ruinous taxation on indigenous industries such as fishing. This rising economic inequality was protected by a large military presence, both Roman and Jewish. Jesus' vision that the Kingdom of God is among you right now is a concrete challenge to both the political and the economic concentration of wealth and power in the hands of a few.

Jesus taught in urban environments, such as on the street and near the Temple, and also in rural and agrarian areas, by the sea or on the side of a hill. It is most likely that, especially in the more rural areas, Jesus' listeners were mostly of the peasant and artisan classes. In Jerusalem, the audience is more a mix of the poor and the elites. Sometimes, as the criticism of the Scribes and the Pharisees indicates, the teaching of Jesus is directed to the poor, but meant to be heard by or repeated to the elites.

The parables are not stories Jesus wrote that he had his followers read and discuss. Parables began as verbal storytelling. People standing or sitting around would have lost interest in the parables if they weren't engaged. They are, in effect, a form of street theatre with a purpose. Parables are often dramatic, and they normally contain an "aha" moment of challenge and discovery. Often, in fact, the parables throw the crowd into a kind of existential crisis. The story has good guys and bad guys, and something isn't right. In a way, those around Jesus stop being listeners and become actors in the story. Indeed, especially with an audience of mixed social and economic classes, the listeners could become actors on opposite sides in the drama. The structure of parables is such that you're challenged to take sides. It's not a question of who Jesus is in the story, as Perkins thinks; it's who *you* are and who the other people in the story are, and what their true roles are in the Kingdom. Then you are challenged to choose sides: God's Kingdom, or Caesar's.

Parables in the ministry of Jesus aren't stories meant to teach by example. Parables, like those we will discuss in the paragraphs that follow, are about reversals. And especially when it comes to issues of money and power, the reversal is always about how the presence of the Kingdom of God turns the power and money relationships of Roman-occupied Israel upside-down.

So, if we don't buy Perkins's free-market capitalist version of the Parable of the Talents, where Jesus (or God) is the investment counselor telling you to make as much spiritual and literal capital as you possibly can and save it for a rainy day, what does this parable mean, in Jesus' time and in our own?

In Jesus' time, a peasant reading of the parable would indeed be a tale of terror, and the third slave admits to being terrified. Suppose, instead of the master representing Jesus or God, he is just as he is portrayed in the parable—a "harsh" man, cruel and exacting, and who, at the end of the tale, actually has the third slave killed. The third slave, the one who is rightly terrified, is the one with whom a peasant audience would identify. He thinks he's being set up, and he's right. In Jesus' time, if you took a deposit from anyone and you lost it, you'd have to face a tribunal and prove you didn't lose it "through malice or intent." The master is throwing around huge sums of money, and if these slaves lose it and can't prove they haven't been negligent, they will have to pay it back. In other words, they will be in debt forever.

To modern readers, some of the drama and terror of the slave in the Parable of the Talents, especially as it is told in Matthew, gets lost because we don't know what a "talent" is. A talent of gold weighed about 30 pounds and was worth about 6,000 denarii. A denarius was one day's wage. In the first century, that's 150 pounds of gold. So, if we translate that into today's money, the master gives the first slave about $2 million. What drama! In story-telling terms, that's "a gazillion dollars."

So the slave is acting honorably and very prudently according to Jewish law.[86] It's the master, a greedy and evil man, who is trying to "reap" where he does not "sow," that is, get a lot of money for which he did basically no work by terrorizing his servants. William Herzog calls the third slave a "whistle-blower" and notes his vulnerability. More than even acting honorably, as Jewish law requires, in the face of this kind of huge exploitation, the third slave has resisted becoming complicit. "He describes the master for what he is and acknowledges his fear of his power. The whistle-blower is no fool. He realizes that he will pay a price, but he has decided to accept the cost rather than continue to pursue his exploitive path."[87]

So, today, the Parable of the Talents could be told like this:

The CEO of an investment firm was going away on a Caribbean vacation, so he went to his youngest investment bankers, newly hired wage slaves struggling to pay off their enormous student loan debt from attending business school. To the first one, he gave $2 million, to the second one he gave $800,000, and to the third one he gave $400,000. Then he went on vacation. The first young banker bought up a lot of sub-prime mortgages, sold them off to an unsuspecting buyer, and doubled the money. The second banker did the same. But the third banker *didn't want to make a quick buck by exploiting unsuspecting buyers, so he hid the money.*

Then the CEO came back. He was thrilled with the profits his first two young hires had made from unsuspecting clients, but he was furious with the third. "Why didn't you exploit the clients?" he asked, outraged. The third young banker replied, "I know you built this company by exploiting people and reaping huge profits, but I found I couldn't do that. I'm a whistle-blower and I reported this firm." So the CEO of the investment firm told him, "You're fired!" And the young banker was cast into the outer darkness of defaulting on his student debt.

Of course, today, banking reform is under heavy pressure. Lobbyists are moving strongly against whistleblower laws that protect those who, like the third slave or the third young banker, expose exploitive investment practices.[88] Modern whistleblowers on the injustices of the current U.S. banking industry can lose their jobs and even be persecuted, our modern version of being "cast into the outer darkness" of the job market, And, like the new business school graduate, they can even be forced to default on student loans because they can't get a job.

THE PLIGHT OF THE DAY LABORER: THE PARABLE OF THE LABORERS IN THE VINEYARD

> *"For the kingdom of heaven is like a landowner who went out early in the morning to hire laborers for his vineyard. After agreeing with the laborers for the usual daily wage, he sent them into his vineyard. When he went out about nine o'clock, he saw others standing idle in the marketplace; and he said to them, 'You also go into the vineyard, and I will pay you whatever is right.' So they went. When*

he went out again about noon and about three o'clock, he did the same. And about five o'clock he went out and found others standing around; and he said to them, 'Why are you standing here idle all day?' They said to him, 'Because no one has hired us.' He said to them, 'You also go into the vineyard.' When evening came, the owner of the vineyard said to his manager, 'Call the laborers and give them their pay, beginning with the last and then going to the first.' When those hired about five o'clock came, each of them received the usual daily wage. Now when the first came, they thought they would receive more; but each of them also received the usual daily wage. And when they received it, they grumbled against the landowner, saying, 'These last worked only one hour, and you have made them equal to us who have borne the burden of the day and the scorching heat.' But he replied to one of them, 'Friend, I am doing you no wrong; did you not agree with me for the usual daily wage? Take what belongs to you and go; I choose to give to this last the same as I gave to you. Am I not allowed to do what I choose with what belongs to me? Or are you envious because I am generous?' So the last will be first, and the first will be last." (Matthew 20:1–16, *New Revised Standard Version*)

This parable is found only in Matthew. While he follows the same narrative as Mark, between Mark 10:1–31 and 32 Matthew inserts the Parable of the Laborers in the Vineyard. Matthew has the parable talk to his location and that of his struggling community, where those who converted or joined became part of the "vineyard," in other words, the community that followed Christ. Thus, the last ones to join, the new converts or Gentiles, would hear this parable as teaching them that they would be "first," and the Jewish people, who were hired first, would be "last." Thus he introduces the parable with the phrase, "the Kingdom of Heaven is like . . ."

But what happens to the parable when the location is not Matthew's struggling community of reformer Jews and new, non-Jewish converts, but those rural areas where Jesus was trying to teach about what happens when the "Kingdom is among you" as he walked around the land of Israel from Judaea up to the Galilee?

The actors in this setting of a field where grapes were grown are not theological types, per Matthew's use, but actual classes of people in the time of Jesus, and they would be easily recognized by Jesus' followers who came out from the fields, or even from the towns and cities, to hear him.[89]

The owner has got to be one of the elites because cultivated land that produces agricultural products was the major way people acquired wealth in Jesus' time. There's a manager, so this is probably a large holding.

But the first curious item that signals something is not quite right in the story is that the owner is directly involved in hiring the day laborers. Why doesn't he use his manager instead? And the owner seems to be a cheapskate, since he hires as few people as possible, and then, because the day is passing and he needs to finish harvesting, he goes back, and then he goes back again and again.

He's arrogant. He comments on the fact that the day laborers, even during harvest time, are standing around "idle." Finally, for these unemployed laborers, this is just a little too much insult. "They said to him, 'Because no one has hired us.'" There is clearly a surplus of workers if the landowner can just go hire whenever he likes and find day laborers still waiting for work at five o'clock. In other words, unemployment is high. The landowner doesn't even need to negotiate with the later hires. He's in control of the situation and he knows it.

But then comes the payout, and the landowner sends the manager to do that. He insults the first hired, who have worked in the hot sun all day, and pays the last ones first. It's an affront, and the first-hired workers know it. Their hard work is not valued; in any case, the "usual wage" for a day laborer in Jesus' time was hardly enough to keep body and soul together. They should get overtime pay, and they don't. There's a casual shaming of their putting in a full day's work in grueling conditions.

And so they protest. Even in such dire economic conditions, where there is clearly a huge surplus of day labor, they dare to raise their voices. "Friend," says the landowner, condescending to one of them, "I can basically do what I want with what is mine." Nothing is said about what is just, what is owned to people who have worked hard. The landowner says, "this belongs to me." All of it. One of the chief clues to the fact that this is not the Kingdom of God "among you," as Jesus taught, is that the parable constantly refers to the "landowner."

In ancient Israel, however, it was commonly believed that the land belonged to God and was God's to distribute. This is the basis of the debt code, where every Jubilee year all debts were cancelled and the land redistributed. This Jubilee concept recognizes a deep truth, namely that the more one accumulates, the more one's desire increases. This eventually becomes the kind covetous greed that destroys community and makes the many into the slaves of a few.[90]

It's also crucial to realize that those who work the land have a deep connection with it. To say that it is owned only by individuals, or even by corporations, and that the workers should have no say in how much they are paid, their overtime, or their health and safety conditions, is an affront to God.

Jesus tells this parable to get those who work the land to recognize how vastly this landowner's viewpoint differs from commonly accepted traditional Jewish belief, that God gives the land and human beings work in community to create abundance for all, that all may live. But now, in Jesus' time, a new system has grown up in which the surplus wealth created in the cities has allowed a small number of the rich to buy up the land and act, in effect, as though they are surrogates for God by virtue of their wealth. This, teaches Jesus through this parable, is not the Kingdom of God.

Here's the crisis in this parable: suppose the land is not really the landowner's, but God's, and it is not the landowner's decision what is just, but God's? How would we organize our agricultural work if we believed that?

CESAR CHAVEZ ON #OCCUPYTHEBIBLE

Cesar Chavez is one of the most famous Latino Americans. With Dolores Huerta, he helped organize the National Farm Workers Association (NFWA), and he understood very well that he not only had to occupy farm labor for the better, he also had to occupy the Bible and his Catholic faith traditions. Chavez said,

> *Jesus' life and words are a challenge at the same time that they are Good News. They are a challenge to those of us*

who are poor and oppressed. By His life He is calling us to give ourselves to others, to sacrifice for those who suffer, to share our lives with our brothers and sisters who are also oppressed. He is calling us to "hunger and thirst after justice" in the same way that we hunger and thirst after food and water: that is, by putting our yearning into practice.[91]

Chavez, Huerta, and the United Farm Workers (UFW) movement had a significant impact not only on the history of American labor, extending it finally into the fields, but also on issues like environmental justice and immigrant rights. Dolores Huerta received the Medal of Freedom from President Obama for her witness for farmworkers, and also for

United Farm Worker supporters marching in Phoenix, Arizona, with Joseph Kennedy III.

Walter P. Reuther Library, Wayne State University, June 4, 1972

women's rights, including protection from domestic violence. Arrested twenty-two times, she was beaten so severely by San Francisco police during a peaceful and legal protest that her spleen ruptured.[92]

The nonviolent practices of Dr. King and the Civil Rights movement, as well as Huerta and Chavez, such as boycotts, marches, and faith-based organizing, were a powerful part of this significant movement.[93] Chavez also used the hunger strike, or fasting, as did Gandhi in India, to great effect. This was a way to physically occupy the biblical text on what it meant to "hunger and thirst after justice" with his own body. He risked his own health to embody what was happening to farm workers' bodies when they toiled in pesticide-laden fields for long hours, sometimes without sufficient water or food.

Protesting farm workers, often out of their Catholic Mexican tradition, carried banners with pictures of Our Lady of Guadalupe, the patron saint of the Mexican downtrodden. Our Lady of Guadalupe has crossed traditions as a symbol of God's presence with the poor and opposed, and it is now also used by Protestants in the American southwest who struggle with immigration and border issues.[94]

THE PARABLE OF THE DAY LABORERS

The Parable of the Workers in the Vineyards, while it draws attention to the plight of farm workers, is also a parable about the vulnerability of today's laborer in an ownership society that does not respect transcendent claims of justice. Gay and transgender Americans, for example, are very vulnerable to workplace discrimination, sexual harassment, and being fired for no reason other than for their sexual orientation or identity.[95] They are denied even existing labor protections for no other reason than because of our society's failure to acknowledge simple human equality.

As labor protections erode rather than improve, many Americans can experience workplace vulnerability today and end up living the plight of the day laborer.

A recent report by Seton Hall Law school called "Ironbound Underground: Wage Theft and Workplace Violations Among Day Laborers in Newark's East Ward" documents the way day laborers in the United States are routinely underpaid, denied overtime, given no benefits, and often abused. The report reveals that 96 percent of local immigrant day laborers have been victims of wage theft, 27 percent have been assaulted by their employers, 80 percent were not given safety equipment, and 20 percent have been hurt on the job.

Day laborers hoping for work in Plainfield, New Jersey.
The Star-Ledger, Newark NJ, 2008

"It's pretty brutal," said Bryan Lonegan, a Seton Hall Law professor, immigration attorney, and co-author of the report. "Day laborers are accepting their fate as a transactional cost for working in the United States."[96]

The stories are indeed testimony to the brutality of the routine exploitations in day labor. For example, a day laborer in Elizabeth, New Jersey, spent two weeks hauling tar in the heat on a roofing job. When it was time to get paid, the contractor refused to give him a dime. When another day laborer from Orange asked why he had not been paid for a landscaping job, his boss punched him and left him on the side of the Garden State Parkway.[97]

That is the consequence to human bodies when an ownership society runs rampant and surplus labor is just there for the taking. The landowner in the Parable of the Workers in the Vineyard may have tried to hire as few workers as possible and then insulted those he did hire and refuse to pay overtime, but he did not assault them. However, their economic vulnerability and that of the day laborer in New Jersey and, indeed, throughout the United States, is the same. They live or die at the caprice of the owner.

JESUS, PARABLES, AND THE FREE MARKET

Of all the kinds of columns I write for the *Washington Post* online, none are as controversial as those where I contrast the biblical message of Jesus with "free-market capitalism." My column "It's not class warfare, it's Christianity"[98] went viral within hours of being posted online, helped by right-wing outrage.[99]

What the free-marketers need to understand, I argue, is that unregulated capitalism, interpreted as God's invisible hand, is completely unbiblical. It's lousy Christianity. But I also argue that free-market capitalism is lousy capitalism because every time capitalism shakes off regulation, it runs the American economy smack dab into a ditch. That's what happened in 1929, and it happened again in 2008.

Conservative religious and political elements in the United States want to convince Americans that Jesus was a free-market capitalist. He wasn't, not by a long shot. But Jesus did have an economic theory, and it's pretty radical. It's called the Jubilee.

6

The Jubilee, or, Jesus Had an Economic Plan

When Jesus came to Nazareth, where he had been brought up, he went to the synagogue on the sabbath day, as was his custom. He stood up to read, and the scroll of the prophet Isaiah was given to him. He unrolled the scroll and found the place where it was written: "The Spirit of the Lord is on me, because he has anointed me to bring good news to the poor. He has sent me to proclaim release to the captives and recovery of sight for the blind, to let the oppressed go free, to proclaim the year of the Lord's favor." (Luke 4:16–19, *New Revised Standard Version*)

Jesus started his ministry by standing up in the synagogue and starting to read. He chose verses from the prophet Isaiah announcing "good news to the poor." This is a reading from that biblical prophet's accounting of the biblical Jubilee, a fifty-year cycle of debt forgiveness, land redistribution, and a cancellation of indentured servitude caused by debt. It's a pretty radical plan for economic equality in a community, not only in early Hebrew history, but also in Jesus' time, and even today.

The text in Luke says that Jesus was given the scroll or book of Isaiah; it seems he chose the verses. After Jesus read the text about "good news to the poor," he sat down, as would be the custom if he were about to preach on the text, interpreting it. Jesus said, "Today this scripture has been fulfilled in your hearing." The congregation of Jesus' hometown folks was, so far, favorably impressed, remarking on how "Joseph's son" spoke very well.

But after that, things didn't go so well. Jesus goes on. He brings the text a little too close to home for his audience. It's all very well to talk vaguely about forgiving debts in the time of the prophet Isaiah, but gradually it starts to dawn on the people in the congregation that Jesus is saying that this biblical practice, in which you were actually supposed to forgive debt, free slaves, and redistribute land, was what he was calling for here and now.

All of a sudden, it wasn't "hometown boy makes good in synagogue" anymore, but "throw the bum out."

> *When they heard this, all in the synagogue were filled with rage. They got up, drove him out of the town, and led him to the brow of the hill on which their town was built, so that they might hurl him off the cliff. But he passed through the midst of them and went on his way.*
> (Luke 4:24–30)

This is, by any account, a very dramatic start to a ministry. From the very beginning of Jesus' public ministry, he didn't just mean to talk about the regular practices of charity;

he meant that the Jews should make concrete changes about issues such as debt, land, and slaves. The people grew so enraged by the idea that they should actually have to do what Isaiah called for in terms of the Jubilee that they tried to kill Jesus.

The Gospels of Matthew, Mark, and Luke all talk about the angry rejection of Jesus by his neighbors in Nazareth, but Luke is most specific, including the quotation from Isaiah. In addition, the quotation from Isaiah that Luke records Jesus reading in the synagogue is really a combination of two different parts of that prophetic text.

Some people ask, "Well, then, did Jesus really read from Isaiah, or not?" since the actual reading is only found in Luke, and it is a composite of texts from Isaiah. It is, however, perfectly plausible that Luke is using a form of the account of Jesus in the synagogue that is simply different from that Mark and Matthew used, and he adapted it to the way he was constructing his Gospel and how he wanted to present it. Remember, Luke's community, as noted before, is a mixed group of wealthy and poor and contains new Gentile members. Thus, Jesus being "run out of the synagogue" and out of town fits with that time of conflict, and Luke wanted to be especially clear about what got the people in the synagogue so enraged.

The rage of the townspeople is an element all three of those Gospels. Jesus clearly did something in the synagogue to make people very angry. What is likely, in fact, is that in his choice of text and his interpretation of that text, Jesus challenged them not to just assume that they were among the privileged of God by virtue of being synagogue-going Jews. A prophetic text of "good news to the poor" announced by

Jesus as happening right now can easily be understood as the trigger for rage so great that a mob became murderously violent. Something really big happened to trouble them. Nothing gets people as upset as hearing that they might lose the money they have lent out and be forced to share the land they own—perhaps for generations—and even let their indentured servants go free. Wealthy people would hear that message as very threatening.

PROCLAIM THE YEAR OF THE LORD'S FAVOR: WHAT EXACTLY IS THE JUBILEE?

The "year of the Lord's favor" is another name for Jubilee. According to Jewish tradition, the Jubilee is a special year of liberty. Every fifty years there is a kind of reboot of Jewish economics and social relations. As described in Leviticus, "And you shall hallow the fiftieth year and you shall proclaim liberty throughout the land to all its inhabitants. It shall be a jubilee for you; you shall return every one of you to your property and every one of you to your family" (25:10). This fiftieth-year (or forty-ninth-year) Jubilee followed seven sabbatical cycles in which every seven years male slaves were released without debt and land was allowed to lie fallow.

In this view, God, not individuals, owns the land, the slaves, and even indentured servants. In Leviticus, God is speaking to Moses: "The land shall not be sold in perpetuity, for the land is mine; with me you are but aliens and tenants" (25:23).

This remarkable understanding of people, God, and property code where male slaves must be released, without debt, after seven years, is based on early Israelite tradition. The Covenant Code (Exodus 21–23) governed how the Jewish people fulfilled their obligations to God, who had established a covenant with them. There is a rough and ready practicality to this code, and an eye-for-an-eye form of justice. The code explains how to deal with economic relations and with lying, thieving, or murder. This is where the early mention of lending at no interest occurs. Then there is the prescribed seven-year cycle after which all male slaves are released without debt (this not true for female slaves). It is bracketed, toward the end of the section, with instruction on letting the land have a "sabbatical year" every seventh year. This is so "the poor of your people may eat" as well as the wild animals (Exodus 23:10). The ritual of the Sabbath rest on the seventh day follows this pattern.[100]

As the Jews became more settled and established a more centralized political structure, they did not abandon the covenant, the sabbatical years, or the Jubilee. But the texts become more specific.

One of the Jubilee texts, Deuteronomy 15:1–6, is about the cancellation of debt, and it is very, very specific.

> *Every seventh year you shall grant a remission of debts. And this is the manner of the remission: every creditor shall remit the claim that is held against a neighbor, not exacting it of a neighbor who is a member of the community, because the LORD's remission has been proclaimed. Of a foreigner you may exact it, but you must remit your claim on whatever any member of your community owes you. There will, however, be no one in need among you . . .*

Some have wondered whether any of this debt forgiveness and release of captives actually took place, but it seems from Deuteronomy 15:7–11 that warnings against creating economic strategies to avoid the sabbath year had to be created. This text cautions that you should not "entertain a mean thought" and not help your neighbor because "the seventh year, the year of remission, is near."

The prophets, like Isaiah, saw the Jubilee year and sabbath years both as a renewal for the Jewish people and a vision of what they could be to one another yet again.

When Jesus starts his public ministry by reading, "The spirit of the Lord GOD is upon me, because the LORD has anointed me; he has sent me to bring good news to the oppressed, to bind up the brokenhearted, to proclaim liberty to the captives, and release to the prisoners; to proclaim the year of the LORD's favor . . ." (Isaiah 61:1–2a), he claims that this vision is being fulfilled "today . . . in your hearing." This clearly means that Jesus was identifying his public ministry with a Jubilee year, when the economic reboot of his society would take place.[101]

JUBILEE TODAY

The good news to the poor and annunciation of the year of the Lord's favor was so controversial for Jesus' hearers that they ran him out of town and tried to kill him. Even so, as I have argued especially in the last two chapters, Jesus continued to see his mission as announcing that the "Kingdom of God is in your midst" and to keep contrasting that reality with the reality of the Roman kingdom of Caesar and the Temple elites who cooperated with it. Evidence from texts on the Jubilee in the Hebrew Bible suggests that it was controversial and difficult to implement; additional measures had to be taken to keep people from sabotaging the intent of the sabbatical year, for example. And this was in a far less complicated agrarian society. But Jesus plainly thought it was not only possible, but also actually necessary to implement in his day.

But how could the biblical Jubilee possibly work as an economic plan in today's economy, one that is far more complicated?

Rising income inequality, increasing debt, and even forms of indentured servitude are on the rise on the United States, and these problems were not created by the economic crisis of 2007. They are problems of much longer standing; the Great Recession just exposed them in a dramatic way.

The national debate continues to be whether austerity, that is, cuts to social programs in the national budget and tax cuts for the rich, are the way out of this crisis, or whether more stimulus spending, increased spending on social programs that benefit the poor and middle class, and taxing the wealthiest is the way out.

Rep. Paul Ryan (R-WI) gave his name to two GOP budgets that would make the massive Bush tax cuts for the rich permanent, raise taxes on the middle class, and cut programs that help the poor. Ryan's philosophical mentor for such a radical economic plan was the philosopher of selfishness, Ayn Rand. Rand, of course, was well-known for her atheism and opposition to religion.[102]

Journalist Jonathan Chait, in the pages of *Newsweek* (April 10, 2011), called Ryan out for launching a "war on the weak" and explained "how the GOP came to view the poor as parasites and the rich as our rightful rulers." According to Chait, "His [Ryan's] citation of Rand was not casual. He's a Rand nut. In the days before his star turn as America's Accountant, Ryan once appeared at a gathering to honor her philosophy, where he announced, 'The reason I got involved in public service, by and large, if I had to credit one thinker, one person, it would be Ayn Rand.' He continues to view Rand as a lodestar, requiring his staffers to digest her creepy tracts."[103]

There is a very clear contrast between the teachings of Jesus of Nazareth, announcing his ministry as the beginning of a new biblical Jubilee year and "good news to the poor," and Ayn Rand, a contrast that Rand herself noted.

According to Rand, where Jesus got off track was in his whole idea that we need to help each other. "There is a great, basic contradiction in the teachings of Jesus," Rand writes. She argues that when Jesus teaches about "the salvation of one's soul," that's individualism and therefore good. But when it comes to ethics, Jesus goes off the rails. Jesus' mistake, according to Rand, is the idea that, "in order to save one's soul, one must love or help or live for others." That, Rand argues, leads to Christianity's "failure."[104]

Ever since Rep. Ryan sponsored draconian budget proposals, budgets that would have slashed essential programs for the poor and given big tax breaks to the rich, Ryan's attachment to the works of Ayn Rand has been in the spotlight.

Rev. Jim Wallis took up the contrast between reading Rand and reading the Bible. He compared her work (and Ryan's budget) to Isaiah, and Wallis called down biblically based wrath on those who make a virtue of crushing the poor. He wrote, "Woe to You, Legislators," and thundered, in the words of the prophet, "Doom to you who legislate evil, who make laws that make victims—laws that make misery for the poor, that rob my destitute people of dignity, exploiting defenseless widows, taking advantage of homeless children. What will you have to say on Judgment Day, when Doomsday arrives out of the blue? Who will you get to help you? What good will your money do you?"[105]

Ryan then defended the 2012 version of his budget as compatible with Catholic social teaching. He told the Christian Broadcasting Network that his Catholic faith had helped shape his budget. "Not so fast," said the American Catholic bishops, who criticized the Ryan budget precisely for its cuts to programs that help the poor, such as food stamps.[106] These bishops roundly rejected Ryan's argument that his budget was based in his Catholic faith, arguing that programs for the poor are essential to the "moral and human dimensions of the federal budget."

It's astonishing, therefore, that NPR's *Morning Edition* reported this as a "debate among Christians" as to whether or not Jesus believed in helping the poor, framing the issue as liberal versus conservative Christian views.[107] It's not at all a liberal versus conservative issue. It's about whether you follow the teachings of Jesus on taking care of the poor, and in the case of Catholic doctrine, moral reasoning based on those teachings; or you follow some other teachings that are not part of the Bible and biblical ethics.

JUBILEE VS. ZOMBIE ECONOMICS

Austerity budgets that cut deeply into social programs that help the middle class and the poor are not just bad biblical ethics; they are really bad economics, too. It turns out that greed isn't good—selfishness is bad for the economy.

Paul Krugman, the Nobel Prize–winning economist, coined the phrase "zombie economics" to describe economic theories like "Reaganomics," which has evolved into what I term "Ryanomics." These economic theories have been proven over and over to be brain dead, that is, to not work at all. Yet, like the undead zombies from films like *Night of the Living Dead*, zombie economics keeps walking around. Krugman first used this catchy description for Reaganomics, the so-called trickle-down theory favored during the presidency of Ronald Reagan. The theory holds that if the rich get richer, it will improve the economy overall because their good fortune will trickle down to the less well off below them on the socio-economic ladder, like water cascading over a series of levels on a fountain. The catchphrase for this theory is "a rising tide lifts all boats." Except, as the well-known investor and proponent of millionaires paying their fair share of taxes (the Buffet Rule), Warren Buffet, commented, all this rising tide of the rich getting richer does is "lift all yachts."

Krugman argued in one of his *New York Times* op eds (April 26, 2012) that the European austerity plans have just made those economies far worse. From "Spain to Latvia, austerity policies have produced Depression-level slumps and Depression-level unemployment . . . So we're now living in a world of zombie economic policies—policies that should have been killed by the evidence that all of their premises are wrong, but which keep shambling along nonetheless. And it's anyone's guess when this reign of error will end."[108]

What we need to do is to pretty much model our economics on "good news to the poor." And the place we need to start, just as Jesus did in announcing the Jubilee, is with debt.

DEBT

So much of our current economic crisis is a debt crisis. Student debt and the mortgage debt crisis, which has lately become a

Protesting student loan debts at an Occupy demonstration in Washington, DC.

Associated Press/Jacquelyn Martin, October 6, 2011

foreclosure crisis, are very much a part of the #Occupy movement as it has evolved from 2011. In fact, student debt has been called the "new front" for the #OWS movement.[109] The new iconic face of #Occupy is the masked Unemployed Super Hero, wearing a cape and a ball and chain marked "Student Loans."

As a nation, we need to start taking student loan debt seriously, both as a troubling moral issue and as a ticking economic time bomb. Student loan debt now exceeds $1 trillion dollars, more than the combined credit card debt of all Americans.[110]

A whole generation of young Americans is at risk because of this excessive borrowing. They choose not to pursue certain job options that could benefit society, such as, for example, going into general practice as a doctor, because a specialization will pay them more and thus help them pay off crippling six-figure medical student loans. Hence, fewer medical students are becoming family practitioners, raising the cost of preventive healthcare.

Students in general fall further and further behind in servicing their debt because many of them are unemployed or underemployed and have no way to keep up with the payments. They delay marriage and starting families; they dare not take the risk of quitting a paying job (if they have one!) and starting their own business to create jobs, and they certainly cannot save to buy a home. They are trapped.

There is no question that debt and debt forgiveness were crucial issues for Jesus, as seen not only in his quoting the Jubilee text from Isaiah, but also in his teaching the disciples to pray, "And forgive us our debts, as we forgive our debtors" (Matthew 6:12). Forgiving debt is a crucial issue as we try to understand what Jesus was teaching about money and its relationship to the Kingdom of God.

Forgiving some of the worst of this student debt is crucial to literally saving this American generation. While not raising the interest rate on student debt is one temporary strategy, it is not a solution. The problem is too big. Some of this student debt needs actual legislation to deal with the whole system, as Robert Applebaum calls for on his website, ForgiveStudentLoanDebt.com.[111]

It will take legislation that covers predatory practices and other changes to the way student loans are structured, such as how interest is compounded. Applebaum also argues persuasively that forgiving student loan debt will stimulate the economy.

The kind of Jubilee equality that Jesus calls for, both from Isaiah and in the Lord's Prayer, can be seen in Applebaum's argument. It is a much-needed Jubilee for the whole American economy, because our whole economic system is tied into this cycle of more student borrowing and mounting student loan debt. Indeed, the conservative-leaning *Economist* (October 29, 2011) asked if student debt is going to be the next big "credit bubble."[112]

Our complicated and interrelated economy actually makes it *more* urgent that we address student debt, not less. What happens to our fragile economy when this next house of cards comes tumbling down?

The #Occupy movement is part of this student debt crisis, in terms of both its goals and those who are driving the movement. I've talked to young people who support the #Occupy movement; they are graduates with two and three degrees and no job. I met some of them on Michigan Avenue, for example, walking the same way I was, toward a jobs rally at #Occupy-Chicago. Each young person had a hand-lettered sign around his or her neck. The signs said simply, $45,240, or $67,125, or even $102,000. They were wearing their outstanding student loan debt around their necks. They were heading to the jobs rally and #OccupyChicago.

These graduates are effectively slaves to their loans.[113] Yet, there are some, such as North Carolina Rep. Virginia Foxx, who chairs the House subcommittee on higher education, who deny that this is a crisis and want to make it an issue of personal accountability, not the systematic gutting of financial support for colleges and universities who have had to raise their tuitions and the virtual elimination of low-income college tuition programs such as Pell grants. Foxx actually said she has "very little tolerance for people who tell me that they graduate with $200,000 of debt or even $80,000 of debt."[114]

But Rep. Foxx did not go to school in this economy. She grew up in an America quite different from the one most Americans now face. There have been three decades or more of increasing income inequality accompanied by rising costs. Debt has made up the difference for many households. Thus, the wealthiest Americans are lending to the poorest

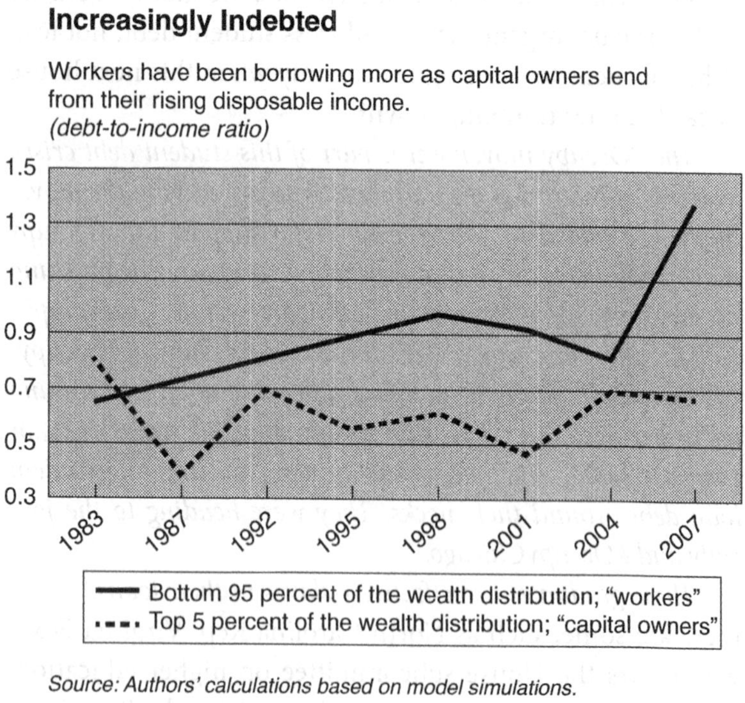

Chart from the International Monetary Fund shows the effect of income inequality on debt.

Michael Kumhof and Romain Rancière/Leveraging Inequality/International Monetary Fund: Finance & Development/December 2010, Vol. 47, No. 4, December 2010

Americans at higher and higher rates. The following chart shows how borrowing has increased as wages have decreased.

Among the factors that led to both the Great Recession and the Great Depression are income inequality; excessive borrowing; too rapid expansion of a poorly regulated financial sector, especially the mortgage lending sector; and a housing bubble that inflated the price of homes. When the weight of risky lending practices hit the wall of not only wage suppression, but also unemployment, the house of cards collapsed.

In the winter and spring of 2012, #OWS also became occupyourhomes.org, a movement to fight foreclosures and evictions. Through coalition building with community organizations, Occupy activists work with homeowners who are at risk of foreclosure, trying to renegotiate their loans and enable families to keep their homes.

But this work needs Jubilee-type legislation. Rep. Keith Ellison (D-Minnesota) has proposed a legislative remedy that has Jubilee written all over it. In February 2012, Ellison released a statement with fellow Congressional Progressive Caucus co-chair Raúl Grijalva (D-Arizona) calling on Freddie Mac and Fannie Mae to write down mortgage principal amounts for homeowners at risk of foreclosure.

This kind of debt forgiveness is another Jubilee approach to our economic crisis that makes practical economic sense. Ellison gave an interview on the idea of debt forgiveness for struggling families.

> *Underwater mortgages are holding people in homes that they can't leave. And if you can't sell your house then you can't go to the job across the nation that might pay more. This is cutting into families' discretionary income. And it's*

a drain on the economy. At the end of the day, we need people to be able to stay in their homes if they want to, and people must be able to sell their homes if they need to. Without writing down these mortgages, we're going to be stuck. I encourage people who are in the housing movement to make a robust and directed demand at the administrator of the Federal Housing Finance Agency (FHFA) [to reduce mortgage principals].[115]

Rep. Ellison is a Muslim, and there is a lot of interesting overlap between the teachings of the Qu'ran on debt forgiveness, the teachings of the Hebrew Bible, and those of Jesus of Nazareth. Islam shows clear support for debt cancellation for those who are unable to meet debt payment; Islam encourages lenders to wait until the loan can be repaid (without penalties). However, for those unable to pay, Islam favors debt forgiveness as a virtuous action, for as the Qu'ran states, "If the debtor is in difficulty, grant him time till it is easy for him to repay. But if ye remit it by way of charity, that is best for you if ye only knew" (2:280).[116]

What is important to see in this context is that not only are religious concepts of Jubilee ethical, they make good economic sense.

RELEASE OF THE CAPTIVES: JUBILEE AND THE PRISON INDUSTRIAL COMPLEX

Jesus announced his ministry by proclaiming good news to the poor, and this included release of the captives. Today, while #OWS has not been active in this area, those who care about biblical justice need to focus their concern on the privatization of prisons and the use of prisoners as effectively slave labor.

Over the last twenty years, the money that states spend on prisons has risen at six times the rate of spending on higher education. In 2011, California spent $9.6 billion on prisons, versus $5.7 billion on higher education. Since 1980, California has built one college campus and 21 prisons. The state spends $8,667 per student per year. It spends about $50,000 per inmate per year.[117]

Just like the situation of my great aunt and the other teenagers with whom she worked in sweatshops in New York's garment district, the rise of the prison industrial complex has returned indentured servitude to the American economic landscape.[118] Prisoners, whose ranks increasingly consist of those for whom the legitimate economy has found no use, now make up a virtual brigade within the reserve army of the unemployed, whose ranks have ballooned along with the U.S. incarceration rate. The Corrections Corporation of America and G4S (formerly Wackenhut), two prison privatizers, sell inmate labor at subminimum wages to Fortune 500 corporations like Chevron, Bank of America, AT&T, and IBM.

The nineteenth century had convict labor, and before that, such prison conditions were called penal colonies. The American economy was built on slave labor, as captive private prison labor is closely coming to resemble. Michelle Alexander points out in her eye-opening book, *The New Jim Crow: Mass Incarceration in the Age of Colorblindness,* "There are more African Americans under correctional control today—in prison or jail, on probation or parole—than were enslaved in 1850, a decade before the Civil War began."[119]

On every level that Jesus proclaims when he opens the scroll, turns to the Jubilee portion of the prophet Isaiah, and announces his ministry, we in the United States need to hear the word of release today. We need to hear the word of release and proclaim the word of release for those crushed by austerity economics, made captive to debt, held subject to wage inequality, and caught up in private prisons to provide cheap labor.

While Americans are not used to having their national budget choices discussed in biblical and theological terms, that is exactly what has happened in recent years.

The real debate on money and debt is whether we follow Ayn Rand and those like her who support a kingdom of Caesar, or the teachings of Jesus of Nazareth and the Kingdom of God.

Not only do we need to follow the money, however; we also need to follow the power if we are to understand what the Kingdom of God looks like in contrast to the kingdom of Caesar. In Jesus' time, as in our own day, one way to follow the power was to track what was happening to women and women's spiritual, economic, and political equality.

7

Jesus and a Woman of Power

Soon afterwards he went on through cities and villages, proclaiming and bringing the good news of the kingdom of God. The twelve were with him, as well as some women who had been cured of evil spirits and infirmities: Mary, called Magdalene, from whom seven demons had gone out, and Joanna, the wife of Herod's steward Chuza, and Susanna, and many others, who provided for them out of their resources. (Luke 8:1–3, *New Revised Standard Version*)

Now after he rose early on the first day of the week, he appeared first to Mary Magdalene, from whom he had cast out seven demons. She went out and told those who had been with him, while they were mourning and weeping. But when they heard that he was alive and had been seen by her, they would not believe it. (Mark 16:9–11, *New Revised Standard Version*)

> *But Mary stood weeping outside the tomb. As she wept, she bent over to look into the tomb; and she saw two angels in white, sitting where the body of Jesus had been lying, one at the head and the other at the feet. They said to her, "Woman, why are you weeping?" She said to them, "They have taken away my Lord, and I do not know where they have laid him." When she had said this, she turned around and saw Jesus standing there, but she did not know that it was Jesus. Jesus said to her, "Woman, why are you weeping? Whom are you looking for?" Supposing him to be the gardener, she said to him, "Sir, if you have carried him away, tell me where you have laid him, and I will take him away." Jesus said to her, "Mary!" She turned and said to him in Hebrew, "Rabbouni!" (which means "Teacher").* (John 20:11–16, *New Revised Standard Version*)

Mary of Magdala was one of Jesus' most famous and most courageous disciples. She was last at the cross (Mark 15:40), after many of the male disciples, like Peter, had fled in fear of their lives. It is clear from both the Markan and Johannine accounts that Mary called the Magdalene was the first person to whom the risen Jesus appears. She is a person of means who was healed by Jesus and who became a supporter of his movement and, clearly, a devoted follower.

Mary is called Magdalene because she was from the town of Magdala in the Galilee. Magdala is located just a couple miles from the sea, up the road from the town of Tiberius. Magdala was excavated in 1971–74, and the ruins of a small synagogue, a water reservoir, and some mosaics were uncovered. One of the mosaics, now on display in Capernaum, depicts an ancient boat with both sails and oars, not unlike the fishing boat uncovered in the Sea of Galilee, as described in the previous chapter.[120] As a Galilean, Mary of Magdala would have been well aware of the ruinous practices of the Romans against the indigenous fishing industry.

But Mary of Magdala, as well as Joanna, the wife of Herod's steward Chuza, and Susanna, who are named in the account in Luke, is not poor. She has the financial wherewithal to support Jesus. Mentioned with her is Joanna, wife of Chuza, the steward to Herod Antipas. This is another indicator that these women were not from among the poor. Herod Antipas inherited the governance of this region when his father, Herod the Great, died in 4 BCE. Herod Antipas was responsible for constructing Tiberius, named for his patron the Roman Emperor Tiberius, on the western shore of the Sea of Galilee. The city, which became his capital, was a center of rabbinic learning. Chuza and Joanna are among the elite members of this society, and Joanna seems to have both the wherewithal and the independence to join the Jesus movement and support it financially.

Mary Magdalene, however, is not only a person of means. Her actions present her as a person of courage and one who takes charge. While the twelve cower behind locked doors (John 20:19) after Jesus is crucified and placed in a grave, Mary Magdalene is up and about before dawn visiting the tomb. Not finding Jesus, she interrogates a person she presumes to be the gardener. More than anything else told about her in the New Testament, this passage reveals her as someone who is accustomed to exercising authority, perhaps as a person of means in her society, but also perhaps as a person who has some spiritual authority derived from following Jesus of

Nazareth. Mary Magdalene interrogates the "gardener" and wants to know if he has taken Jesus' body away. If so, she says, *she* will take charge of the body and "take him away." It is not until the very personal calling of her name, "Mary," that she recognizes Jesus because she knows him as her teacher.

Not only then is Mary Magdalene a powerful woman, she also had one of the closest and most significant of human relationships with Jesus, that of student and teacher.

After talking with the risen Jesus, Mary Magdalene goes to tell the cowering disciples that Jesus is alive and well. They don't believe her. That this New Testament account has been preserved is doubly surprising. First, women at that time were not considered capable of legal testimony in a court of law. Second, after this remarkable feat of recognizing the risen Jesus and reporting that he was alive to the disciples, Mary Magdalene disappears from the New Testament. She is not mentioned in the Book of Acts, or in any of the epistles. The Apostle Paul records witnesses to the resurrection and manages to include himself, even though his vision on the Damascus road happens after Jesus has ascended, but he conspicuously does not mention Mary Magdalene by name in the list (1 Cor. 15:1–8).

Why, after the prominence of Mary Magdalene in the central moments of Jesus' life, death, and resurrection, does she disappear in the mission of the Jesus movement?

The answer is she doesn't disappear. She just disappears from the New Testament. Extrabiblical literature shows that she subsequently becomes a missionary in spreading the good news about Jesus in his life, death, and resurrection—a rival missionary, perhaps, to both Peter and Paul. The *Gospel of Mary*, written in the second century

CE and discovered in the nineteenth century, has received scholarly attention in the twenty-first century.[121] Karen L. King examines this incredible text in her wonderful work *The Gospel of Mary of Magdala: Jesus and the First Woman Apostle.*[122] This long-lost Gospel presents a convincing argument for women's religious leadership in the early church. It is also a sharp critique of illegitimate power and a vision for spiritual growth. And all of it is written in the name of a woman.

WOMEN "#OCCUPYTHEBIBLE"

Occupying the Bible was a key part of the women's movement for equality from the nineteenth century onward. In 1895 and 1898, Elizabeth Cady Stanton, the famous abolitionist and suffragist, brought together a revising committee of twenty-six women, who published a biblical commentary in two-parts. Their purpose was to challenge the Christian orthodoxy, which used biblical texts to oppose equal rights for women. The commentary is critical in many respects of the treatment of women, but the New Testament passages on Jesus and women are held up as models for a more egalitarian view. The Apostle Paul, however, received little praise.[123]

The next phase of occupying the Bible in regard to gender began in the 1970s. In 1971, Leonard Swidler published his influential essay "Jesus Was a Feminist" in *The Catholic World.* Swidler was, at the time, a member of the religion department at Temple University.[124] The work was part of the new biblical scholarship that was emerging in the period. But what Swidler did was establish the view that "Jesus was a feminist" in the minds of many, a view that, at least in the form of "Jesus treated women as equals," continues in many church circles today.

The most influential work by women in this early period was by Nancy Hardesty and Letha Scanzoni. Their book *All We're Meant to Be: A Biblical Approach to Women's Liberation* was published in 1974.[125] These two evangelical women wanted to demonstrate that the Bible, and especially the New Testament, actually liberates women.

But while evangelical women's work was accepted and even praised into the early 1980s, women's work on occupying the Bible went in different directions after the 1970s. One direction could be termed "radical," as the work of Mary Daly exemplifies. Daly ultimately concluded that the Christian scriptures are so riddled with patriarchy that they are unredeemable for supporting women's wholeness and integrity.[126]

The other direction is a reformist approach, illustrated especially by formidable New Testament scholar Elisabeth Schussler Fiorenza. In her work *In Memory of Her*, published in 1983, Schussler Fiorenza uses the historical-critical method of biblical scholarship to reconstruct early Christian origins and to show that Jesus of Nazareth stood in judgment against the marginalization of women. Female subordination in the New Testament is, instead, an accommodation of Christianity to the Greco-Roman world as it spread.[127] Schussler Fiorenza concludes, "Only those traditions and texts that critically break through patriarchal culture . . . have the theological authority of revelation." Significantly, Fiorenza finds "such revelation . . . in the life and ministry of Jesus as well as in the *discipleship community of equals* called forth by him."[128]

Schussler Fiorenza's clear view from below of how to interpret the Bible in light of the patriarchal oppression of women is a helpful corrective to the earlier affirmation of Jesus and his frequent contact with women as portrayed in the Gospels, especially in Luke. Luke has sometimes been called the "women's Gospel" because many women appear in the text. But as New Testament scholar Sharon Ringe has pointed out, a great many of these stories about women show them in "very traditional roles played by women in the Hellenistic world of the Roman empire." This is Luke's audience, as he was writing to a diverse group of both well-to-do and poorer people, both Jews and Gentiles, perhaps living at a considerable distance from Palestine after the Roman-Jewish war of 66–70.[129] So, while a lot of stories in Luke feature women, quantity is not necessarily quality.

Luke, on the one hand, is trying to convince his wealthier audience to see the good news of Jesus' life, death, and resurrection as challenging the contemporary social order. But that means, says Ringe, that sometimes Luke pulls his punches, not only on issues of gender, but also on wealth and poverty.

There is a critique of elitist power, but today we "have to acknowledge that a dangerous Roman imperial rhetoric seems to have shaped Luke's vision."[130] Thus, the economic critique that Ringe emphasizes, and the critique of patriarchal power that Schussler Fiorenza provides, help us see that the "Jesus was a feminist" way of occupying the Bible on gender is not sufficient.

African American women have delved into scripture as *womanists*, a term that means "a black feminist or feminist of color" as defined by Alice Walker.[131] Dealing with the triple oppressions of race, gender, and class, African American women do biblical interpretation, as well as theology, ethics, pastoral care, and ministry, through these complex lenses. While white women, such as Ringe and Schussler Fiorenza, have drawn attention to the gender and economic issues in the Bible, womanists have gone even deeper into the struggles of women of color, both in the text and in living out of the text. Renita Weems occupies scripture on these triple oppressions, particularly in regard to violence against women.[132] The womanist way of reading scripture is profoundly different from that of many feminists, as Jacqueline Grant's book title, *White Women's Christ, Black Women's Jesus: Feminist Christology and Womanist Response*,[133] so well illustrates.

Womanist biblical interpretation[134] challenges me and should challenge all Christians who are serious about occupying scripture to learn what Jesus really said about money and power, to recognize that an analysis of racial discrimination, along with gender and economic discrimination, is indispensible. The depth of the challenge of Jesus of Nazareth to his own time, and ours, will never be adequately understood without this triple lens of race, gender, and economics.

This triple oppression is absolutely critical to understanding how power suppresses those on the margins in order to control. That is what makes the relationship of Jesus of Nazareth and Mary Magdalene so significant. Mary Magdalene was a woman of power in terms of both economic influence and gender equality in the Jesus movement. She was Jesus' friend and his student during his ministry, and she was his apostle after his death and resurrection. For that very reason, she was framed by the church in a way that suppressed her power.

MARY MAGDALENE WAS FRAMED

Mary Magdalene, last at the cross and first at the tomb, the friend of her teacher, Jesus of Nazareth, is now mostly remembered as the most famous prostitute in history. Why?

The reason is that the early medieval church trashed Mary Magdalene's reputation as an apostle, that is, as a resurrection witness, and deliberately made her into a prostitute.

Toward the end of the sixth century, Pope Gregory the Great "preached a homily . . . that established a new Magdalen for western Christendom."[135] The Pope proclaimed, "'We believe that this woman [Mary Magdalen] whom Luke calls a female sinner, whom John calls Mary, is the same Mary from whom Mark says seven demons were cast out.' In other words, Gregory collapsed into one individual the identities of three distinct women described in the gospels."[136]

Donatello's haunting and powerful sculpture of Mary Magdalene.
© 2006 Mary Ann Sullivan, 2006

The Pope identified Mary of Magdala, a woman who figures prominently in the crucifixion and resurrection stories, as a whore. There is absolutely no evidence for this identification in the New Testament.

As I have written on the defamation by the Church of the Magdalene as a repentant prostitute,

"It was a way to exclude women from religious leadership in the Jesus movement."[137]

The movie industry has picked up where the medieval Church left off. In an essay on the Magdalene in five contemporary films, particularly Franco Zeffirelli's *Jesus of Nazareth* (1977) and Martin Scorsese's *The Last Temptation of Christ* (1988), Jane Schaberg observes "[E]ach film's Magdalene is the conflated figure of . . . the repentant whore."

But perhaps the most recent damning (meant in both senses, that is, both critical and damned to hell) film portrayal of Mary Magdalene is in Mel Gibson's *The Passion of The Christ*. This was the remarkably violent movie on the death of Jesus of Nazareth made by Mel Gibson. It earned an R rating for the violence, and conservative Christian churches, flocking to the film, often bringing young children, made it the highest-grossing R-rated movie of all time.

The Gibson version of the passion narratives of the New Testament takes enormous license with the biblical texts. It is, itself, an effort to occupy scripture, reversing the kind of critical biblical scholarship discussed earlier. This is, as Gibson himself so frequently said, an effort to establish truth. As an interpretation of the New Testament as a violent struggle between God and the Devil over the broken and bruised body of Jesus of Nazareth, it is a stretch. But it is scarcely the truth.

An example would be the hatchet job Gibson does on Mary Magdalene. Not content with Pope Gregory's confusions of Mary Magdalene with the "woman of the city," Gibson identifies her as the woman about to be stoned in the text most scholars conclude is a later addition to the Gospel of John, 7:53–8:11. It is a text that has nothing to do with Mary Magdalene.

But in Gibson's heroic tale of Jesus, there must be a girl to save, and what better than to save a fallen woman? The movie portrays this as a flashback to a dusty street scene. Suddenly, a hostile crowd appears. The Jesus figure, his face steely with Clint Eastwood–like resolve, stares down the menacing crowd and then bends down to draw in the dust. Straightening up, Jesus then stands tall as the camera pans up the back of his legs, a direct visual reference to *High Noon*, when Gary Cooper faced down evil in the dusty streets of a western town. Stones drop from the hands of the hostile crowd, and a hauntingly beautiful woman, the actress who plays Mary Magdalene in the rest of the film, raises her anguished face, bruised and cut from stones already thrown, and then crawls through the dust to grasp Jesus' feet.

Mel Gibson does to Mary Magdalene basically the same thing the sixth-century church did, mistakenly calling her a prostitute and effectively undercutting her spiritual authority. It is unsurprising that, in a period of Christian reactionary backlash against women's equality, the lie that Mary Magdalene was a prostitute would recur.

But further connections need to be made among Jesus, gender, and race in sexual shaming. Lorraine Hansbury (1930–1965) was an African American author and playwright. Her best-known work, *A Raisin in the Sun*, was based on her family's experience of racial segregation in Chicago. But Hansbury also knew well the links between Jesus, gender, and race. As she noted so astutely in her informal autobiography, *To Be Young, Gifted and Black*, "You could be Jesus in drag, but if you're brown they're sure you're selling."[138] This insight from Hansbury lets us see that in the eyes of the Roman-born Pope Gregory, Mary Magdalene would not only have been target for sexual shaming because she was a woman who dared to study and missionize, but also because she was a native-born woman—a woman of color.

THE WAR ON WOMEN THEN AND NOW

Rush Limbaugh, the conservative radio talk show host, attempted to silence women's voices in the public square through sexual shaming, not unlike Pope Gregory or Mel Gibson. In the contentious 2012 presidential election season, Limbaugh called Sandra Fluke, a Georgetown University law student and articulate spokeswoman for women's reproductive healthcare, a "slut," a "prostitute," and worse, causing a firestorm of social media–driven protest.

But today, women are not Mary Magdalene, demeaned by church authority and made into the poster woman for the repentant prostitute. Women and their male allies fought back against Limbaugh's attempts to use sexual shaming to silence women citizens. Over 140 of Limbaugh's advertisers quit his program.[139]

New media played an important role. A Facebook page led the boycott, and the use of the Twitter hash tag #StandwithSandra drove the message.[140]

This and similar incidents gave rise to the term "the Republican War on Women" as an issue in the 2012 political season. But the real war on women is not a war of words, though words can be harmful and clearly are not irrelevant. Whether in the time of Luke or in the time of Limbaugh, the real war on women is economic.

Even contraception is, at a basic level, an economic issue for women. Having reliable access to birth control boosts women's wages.[141] The connection between poverty and reproductive issues is made over and over in the attacks on Planned Parenthood. This could be clearly seen when the Susan G. Komen for the Cure foundation attempted to pull funding from Planned Parenthood. The huge backlash against Komen was due in large part because conservatives were (and still are) willing to destroy Planned Parenthood's crucial care for low-income women on preventative health issues such as cervical and breast cancer screening, testing for HIV and other sexually transmitted diseases, and even abstinence counseling for teenagers. Planned Parenthood is frequently where women of color go for their healthcare needs.[142]

All of these issues come together around a woman's economic power and equality. You can't work if you can't regulate the spacing of your children, you can't work if you are dying from preventable diseases, and you can't work if you're sick. Women still make only 81 cents on the male dollar; that's $431,000 less in wages over a forty-year career. Women of all races may make up half the country's population, but they hold only 16 percent of the congressional seats. Women originally lost fewer jobs in the recent recession, but men have gained back more jobs in the better-paying sectors.[143]

WOMEN AND #OWS

#OWS has not been a women's paradise, and sexual assaults and harassment have occurred.[144] The goals of #OWS are about the redistribution of power, especially economic power, but some in the movement have not translated that into gender and racial oppression in terms of their analysis or action.

On the other hand, women who have taken part in street protest movements for a long time note a difference between #OWS and previous protests. Jackie DiSalvo, a City University of New York professor and a member of the #Occupy-WallStreet labor working group, hears what younger women are saying about harassment, but she notes the difference. "I was in SDS [Students for a Democratic Society]—we had all these ego-tripping superstars. There was very macho leadership, and very aggressive sectarian fighting." Now, she adds, "there's really a big effort to avoid domination."

Shaista Husain, also interviewed regarding gender and #OWS, quoted womanist poet and writer Audre Lorde: "Liberation is not the private province of any one particular group." According to Husain, women, people of color, and

Demonstrator at Occupy Wall Street explains the movement.
Timothy Krause (www.flickr.com/photos/33498942@N04/), October 17, 2011

working-class people have been part of the occupation from the beginning. "It wasn't just *Adbusters* and Anonymous calling this occupation from out of nowhere," she says. "It came from Bloombergville and CUNY students: working-class, multicultural students with a connection to labor history."[145]

Rita Nakashima Brock of Faith Voices for the Common Good, an experienced activist and academic with whom I wrote a book on prostitution in Asia and the United States,[146] reports a similar difference at #OccupyOakland.

"The younger men are not the kind of males I demonstrated with in my generation who tended to ignore or shove the females aside. And the women exhibit confidence—I saw quite a number of courageous women calling for nonviolence and standing up to angry men. At one point, when I wanted to ask Dan Siegel a question, I was too short to be seen and too far back to be heard, so I asked my question to a tall young white man standing next to me, thinking he might ask it. Instead, he pressed politely several times, saying 'this lady has a good question; let her ask it.' And I got my chance."[147]

There is improvement. More is needed.

JESUS TRAINED MARY MAGDALENE FOR A JOB

So, in sum, what stands out from #OccupytheBible on women and power is that until the leadership structure of the #Occupy movement fully addresses its own misogyny, structured as it may be by race and class, the kind of economic and social transformation the movement envisions will not be realized.

That is why it is so crucial to highlight Mary Magdalene's importance to Jesus of Nazareth. Jesus of Nazareth and Mary of Magdala traded services: he healed her illnesses, and she used her money to support his movement. Jesus trained her for a job as his student. After his death, Mary Magdalene took the job for which she had been trained. She became a missionary, telling the good news of Jesus' ministry.

But her leadership was sexually demeaned over and over again as the church and popular media repeated the lie that she was a repentant whore. Today women (and men who are supportive of women's equality) who #OccupytheBible need to know this biblical truth: Jesus trained Mary Magdalene for a job, and she did it. She did it so well the patriarchy of the early church felt threatened by her, and in retaliation they sexually shamed her.

Today, the main driver of the so-called war on women is economic, and that economic exploitation has specific race and class dimensions. When we occupy the Bible on issues of gender, race, and class, we need to remember a woman of power who did the job and have the courage to do it, too. You can't occupy just a little bit. You need to go all the way, or you won't succeed.

8

Jesus Against Rome: The Crucifixion of Power

In the fifteenth year of the reign of Emperor Tiberius, when Pontius Pilate was governor of Judea, and Herod was ruler of Galilee . . . during the high priesthood of Annas and Caiaphas, the word of God came to John son of Zechariah in the wilderness . . . John said to the crowds that came out to be baptized by him, "You brood of vipers! Who warned you to flee from the wrath to come? Bear fruits worthy of repentance . . . And the crowds asked him, "What then should we do?" In reply, he said to them, "Whoever has two coats must share with anyone who has none; and whoever has food must do likewise." Even tax collectors came to be baptized, and they asked him, "Teacher what should we do?" He said to them, "Collect no more than the amount prescribed for you." Soldiers also asked him, "And we, what should we do?" He said to them, "Do not extort money from anyone by threats or

> *false accusation . . ."* (Luke 3:1–2, 7, 10–14a, *New Revised Standard Version*)

> *Herod said, "John I beheaded; but who is this about whom I hear such things?"* (Luke 9:9, *New Revised Standard Version*)

> *So Pilate . . . , after flogging Jesus, he handed him over to be crucified.* (Mark 15:15, see also Matthew 27:26, *Luke 23:16, New Revised Standard Version*)

> *Then the soldiers led him into the courtyard of the palace (this is, the governor's headquarters); and they called together the whole cohort . . . Then they led him out to crucify him.* (Mark 15:16, 20b, *New Revised Standard Version*)

Conservative Christians occupy the message of the crucifixion of Jesus, that is, they take possession of its meaning, by claiming that God sent Jesus to die to atone for our sins. In its most severe forms, as seen, for example, in Mel Gibson's *The Passion of the Christ*, all of Jesus' life and teaching are completely subordinate to the fact that he was sent by God to suffer and die. In Gibson's movie, Jesus' Sermon on the Mount lasts less than *40 seconds*, while Jesus is flogged, from beginning to end, for *40 minutes*.

The idea that God sent Jesus to die to atone for our sins is often called the penal theory of the atonement. It is important to realize that this view of the meaning of Jesus' suffering and death was not the view of any of the Church fathers from the period of the early church, that is, the first three centuries

CE, when Christians were persecuted by the Roman Empire. After Christianity became the official religion of the Empire of Constantine in the fourth century, the idea that God sent Jesus to die to pay for our sins started to appear, reaching a high point with Anselm of Canterbury. It was then picked up by the Protestant Reformers, and thus passed into contemporary conservative Christian views.

There are many problems with this theological perspective. One is that it is basically "divine child abuse." It makes God the author of the violence done to Jesus. This view of what Jesus accomplished takes the positive ethical message he taught to his disciples and turns it toward crucifixion as "redemptive suffering."[148]

The idea that suffering is redemptive lies at the root of much of the religious justification of the battering of women by their husbands and partners. I have had so many women tell me that when they finally got up the courage to tell their pastors that their husbands were beating them, those pastors told them to "go home, be a better wife, and forgive him as Christ forgave you from the cross."

And the beatings continued, and often got worse.

In addition, the idea that Jesus was sent by God to die because God demanded a perfect sacrifice to pay for human sin keeps us from paying attention to what actually got Jesus killed and who killed him. Jesus was killed for what he did on earth. Furthermore, he was killed not by the Jews, but by the Romans.

Centuries of murderous anti-Semitism have been justified by the misreading of the biblical text on the death of Jesus. Yes, there was conflict among Jewish parties in Israel, and Jesus himself directly challenged the Jewish elites, both the landowners and the religious authorities in Jerusalem. The Gospels were, as was stated in previous chapters, composed after the destruction of the Temple and after the Jesus movement, when intra-Jewish strife over the future direction of Judaism was combined with fear of further violence from the Roman occupiers.

But when we occupy the Bible on the crucifixion, it becomes clear that it was the Romans, not the Jews, who actually killed Jesus, like they killed John the Baptist before him. The reason the Romans killed Jesus also becomes clearer. The Romans killed Jesus because the movement he was leading was a threat to their military and economic control of the region.

THE POWER OF ROME

Jesus was not the only Jewish reformer to be killed by the Romans in Palestine during the early first century CE. John the Baptist, who came out of the wilderness and preached wrath against Herod, the Roman ruler of the Galilee, was arrested by Herod and eventually put to death. John, like Jesus, advocated living according to the Kingdom of God, not the kingdom of Caesar. The Kingdom of God was not only in the future for John; in his teaching, present-day relations among people need to change, as in the text cited at the beginning of this chapter. John's program was pretty similar to that of Jesus of Nazareth: take care of the poor among you, and don't exploit people. Tax collectors and soldiers were even beginning to listen to John the Baptist, the two sources of control an occupying power needs—the military and the people who supplied the money. Herod had him beheaded.

Jesus of Nazareth taught in his hometown that there was about to be "good news for the poor" through the Jubilee debt cancellation and land redistribution. Then he went up to the Galilee, recruited followers from among those whose fishing business was being taxed out of existence by the Romans, taunted the legendary might of the Roman legions (calling them demons and comparing them with pigs!), taught women to be leaders in his movement, sided with peasants against landowners in practices of day labor and wage manipulation, and advocated that slaves become whistleblowers when their masters tried to make them collaborate in the practice of lending out money at high interest rates. Then Jesus went to the Temple in Jerusalem, during the peak time of Passover, and overturned the tables of the moneychangers. That seems to have tipped the hand of the ruling powers. But indeed, it's a miracle Jesus wasn't killed sooner by the Romans, who had a habit, as with John the Baptist, of killing those who would upset their rapidly expanding military and commercial enterprises.

While the Gospels record the events leading up to the crucifixion of Jesus and the aftermath from their different perspectives on the meaning of that event, several things are clear. Jesus was crucified by the Romans; Roman soldiers whip Jesus and then carry out the actual crucifixion. Jesus was accused of *both* a religious crime (blasphemy), and a civil crime (sedition). But the chief priests and scribes of the Temple, who no doubt wanted to have Jesus eliminated for his direct challenge not only to their religious teachings but also to their lucrative Temple businesses, did not have the power. Rome had the ultimate power of violence, the power to put people to death.

Rome actually had more to lose than the Temple elites, in fact, if the people started to follow the program of Jesus of Nazareth, what he called the Kingdom of God, and refused to follow the kingdom of Caesar. As I said in Chapter 1, "Reading the Bible from the Streets." Who is more dangerous to the Romans, the violent insurrectionist Barabbas, or the nonviolent revolutionary Jesus of Nazareth? The Romans understood violence, and they knew how to deal with it. They were a military power. But nonviolence is confounding and threatening to an occupying power because you literally can't have a soldier for every person you are trying to control. People have to obey, or you lose.

It is clear, then, that the Romans killed Jesus of Nazareth. As the historian Josephus records this sequence of events, Pilate, the ruthless governor of Judea, is the one who has Jesus crucified.

> *About this time there lived Jesus, a wise man . . . For he was one who wrought surprising feats and was a teacher of such people as accept the truth gladly. He won over many Jews and many of the Greeks . . . When Pilate, upon hearing him accused by men of the highest standing among us, had condemned him to be crucified, those who had in the first place come to love him did not give up their affection for him . . .* (Josephus, *Jewish Antiquities 18:63*)

All the Gospels record that Jesus was flogged before he was crucified. This is another indication that it is a Roman execution. The traditional Jewish method of execution was stoning. The Romans, however, routinely had people brutally flogged before crucifixion, as Josephus again records. "They were whipped, their bodies were mutilated, and while they were still alive and breathing, they were crucified" (*Jewish Antiquities* 12:256).

The fury of the Roman soldiers when putting down the Jewish armed insurrection that included the Roman destruction of the Temple should leave no doubt about what the Romans were capable of when their power was threatened.

"They [the Jewish insurrectionists] were accordingly scourged and subjected to torture of every description, before being killed, and then crucified opposite the walls . . . five hundred or sometimes more being captured daily. . . . The soldiers out of rage and hatred amused themselves by nailing their prisoners in different postures; and so great was their number, that space could not be found for the crosses nor crosses for the bodies." (Josephus, *Jewish War* 5:446–51)

Torture before execution was one of the hallmarks of the Roman method of exercising tyrannical power.

TORTURE: THE ULTIMATE ABUSE OF POWER

On May 4, 2004, graphic pictures of prisoners being tortured at the now infamous U.S. military–controlled Abu Ghraib prison raced around the world.

What the world saw was the face of the United States, not as the symbol of freedom and democracy, but as a nation turned rogue state, like Argentina under its military junta, South Africa under Apartheid, or Germany in the Nazi era. The United States was pursing a systematic practice of torture against prisoners, justified by a series of confidential legal memos. These memos developed a spurious line of legal

Staged Abu Ghraib image from the set of *Standard Operating Procedure* by Errol Morris.

Nubar Alexanian, June 2008

argument that was supposed to prove that the United States did not have to follow the Geneva Conventions in the case of enemy combatants.[149]

Jane Mayer, who as a journalist and writer for *The New Yorker* doggedly pursued these memos, documented that the torture was, from the beginning, not the work of a 'few bad apples,' but administration policy at the highest levels.[150]

The use of torture post 9/11 was not about getting information to protect America. Many experienced military and clandestine services operators have gone on record arguing that torture doesn't work to get good information and thus keep the nation safer. In fact, Daniel Coleman, an ex-FBI agent who worked closely with the CIA, said, "Brutalization doesn't work. We know that. Besides, you lose your soul."

Instead, torture is all about the abuse of power. That's what the Romans knew, and why they would routinely torture those about to be crucified. It was to produce an excess of pain in order to control, to destroy one world and create another. That is the point Elaine Scarry so brilliantly argues in her book *The Body in Pain: The Making and Unmaking of the World*. An example Scarry uses, and a good example since most people can relate to it, is what happens when the dentist's drill accidentally hits a nerve in your tooth. You see stars. What that simply means is that everything else in your life, your memory, your experience, your whole being is obliterated and you become reduced to that world-destroying pain.[151]

Scarry says that torture is employed by political regimes as a "spectacle of power." What actually happens, however, is that the regime is revealed as "so unstable, that torture is being used." In other words, torture, as systematic brutality, is supposed to look like power, but that is a fiction. It isn't power. What torture exposes is that when a political power resorts to torture to exercise its power, it is actually doing so because it is weak and unstable.[152] This kind of political power is really a hall of mirrors, a fun-house distortion of genuine political power based on strong values of community and justice.

Manadel al-Jamadi, whose "iced corpse" was one of the photos circulated from Abu Ghraib, died after interrogation, and his death was ruled a homicide. The pathologists who conducted the autopsy, according to Jane Mayer, noted the "compromised respiration" and "blunt force injuries" to Jamadi's head and torso. But they were apparently "unaware that Jamadi had been shackled to a high window." When chief forensic pathologist for the State of New York Dr. Michael Baden reviewed the autopsy report, he noted that the hanging from the high window was significant. "He [Jamadi] also had injuries to his ribs. You don't die from broken ribs. But if he had been hung up in this way and had broken ribs, that's different." In the doctor's view, "asphyxia is what he died from—as in a crucifixion."[153]

The United States, under a new administration, has taken steps to once again abide by the Geneva Conventions and refrain from torture. Yet, there has not been a full investigation of this earlier period, and neither those who authorized the torture of prisoners nor those who carried it out have, in the main, been brought to justice.

In 2012, respected senior journalist Bill Moyers argued that Memorial Day was an appropriate time to reflect on the fact that as a nation we had engaged in torture and not yet dealt with it. "So here we are, into our eleventh year after 9/11, still at war in Afghanistan, still at war with terrorists, still at war with our collective conscience as we grapple with how to protect our country from attack without violating the basic values of civilization—the rule of law, striving to achieve our aims without corrupting them, and restraint in the use of power over others, especially when exercised in secret."[154]

The United States will not be confident again in its values, either at home or abroad, unless we work this through as a nation.

The death by crucifixion of Jamadi, as well as all the other torture that occurred during this period, happened because the United States felt weak and vulnerable. Jane Mayer titles her first chapter "Panic." Power that tortures is not supremely powerful; it is actually weak at its core.

POWER AND DOMESTIC POLICING

A disturbing power shift has occurred in the United States post 9/11, revealed not only in the resort to torture of enemy combatants, but also in the militarization of domestic police forces. This militarization of police began during the "war on drugs" that has filled our private prisons with so many Americans, a disproportionate number of them African Americans. It has escalated with the "war on terror," and the Supreme Court's 2012 decision to uphold sections of Arizona's controversial immigration act allowing police to demand papers from anyone they consider suspiciously not American, and the net effect is that police forces adopt military strategies.

These strategies are now being used to control ordinary citizens exercising their first amendment rights. This fear-based potential abuse of power reveals a troubling weakness of American power. When a democracy does not trust its citizens, it can cease being a democracy. And when the super rich buy their own government by secretly—and not so secretly—corrupting the democratic process by pouring unequalled amounts of money into it to get their own way, regardless of the wishes of the majority, the democracy becomes a plutocracy.

This book has described the use of pepper spray against peacefully protesting students at the University of California Davis. Police tear-gassed the Occupy protestors in Oakland, California, and the nighttime raid on Zuccotti Park that ousted the encampment there was carried out like a military operation, with klieg lights and a military-type sound machine.

The Posse Comitatus Act of 1878, still in force, was "passed to prevent U.S. military personnel from acting as law enforcement agents on U.S. soil."[155] But today, the merging of military style tactics, funding for "anti-terror" work, and even enormous amounts of equipment such as tanks and full body armor are common for police.

These developments can be easily seen in the cultural lens of television. The program *24* premiered in November of 2001 and ended in 2010. It starred Kiefer Sutherland as Jack Bauer, the head of a counter-terrorism unit. The show featured at least one torture scene per episode, a remarkable statistic since each show covered *only one day*. This torture included shooting "terrorists" in the kneecap, chopping off their hands, or even biting them to death. It proved remarkably effective in convincing Americans that torture was justified to "save American lives."

But the equivalent for the question of the militarization of policing is the popular show *Hawaii Five-O*. It is a police procedural that premiered in 2010 based on the original *Hawaii Five-O* of nearly forty years earlier. The episodes featured investigations of crimes and a successful arrest. Most of the original *Hawaii Five-O* shows ended with the head investigator, Steve McGarrett, sharply ordering his second in command, Danny Williams, "Book'em, Dano," a phrase that entered the popular culture.

If you compare the original show, still frequently aired in reruns, to the new version, you will see the enormous escalation of militarized-style policing. In fact, the conflict over a militarized police response, including a too-aggressive use of force, is part of the new show itself. The character who plays Danny Williams, Dano from the original, is a regular cop from New Jersey who wants to do things by the book. Lieutenant Commander Steve McGarrett, who is a former

Navy Seal, frequently goes rogue with an ends-justify-the-means approach, using excessive force both in hand-to-hand combat, and with a huge array of weapons. Dano is not always successful at stopping him.

The post-9/11 militarization of the police is mirrored in this popular show. Radley Balko, a journalist who has studied the issue, has written that in 2009, stimulus spending was used to "fund militarization, with police departments requesting federal funds for armored vehicles, SWAT armor, machine guns, surveillance drones, helicopters, and all manner of other tactical gear and equipment."[156]

Experienced police officers themselves find this incredibly alarming, even tragic. Former Seattle Police Chief Norm Stamper has said as much. "We needed local police to play a legitimate, continuing role in furthering homeland security back in 2001," says Stamper, now a member of Law Enforcement Against Prohibition. "After all, the 9/11 terrorist attacks took place on specific police beats in specific police precincts. Instead, we got a ten-year campaign of increasing militarization, constitution-abusing tactics, needless violence, and heartache as the police used federal funds, equipment, and training to ramp up the drug war. It's just tragic."[157]

As the *New York Times* reported, "such tactics are used in New York City, where Police Commissioner Raymond W. Kelly (whose department has had armored vehicles for decades) has invoked both the nineteenth-century military strategist Carl von Clausewitz and the television series *24* in talking about the myriad threats his city faces—both conventional and terrorist. After the would-be Times Square bomber Faisal Shahzad was arrested aboard a plane at Kennedy Airport in 2010, Mr. Kelly calculated the plot-to-capture time: slightly more than fifty-three hours.

"Jack Bauer may have caught him in twenty-four," said Mr. Kelly, who served as a Marine commander in Vietnam. "But in the real world, fifty-three's not bad."[158]

A militaristic mind-set is creeping into officers' approach to their jobs, said Timothy Lynch, director of the criminal justice project at the Cato Institute, a libertarian think tank. "It is in the way they search and raid homes and the way they deal with the public," he said. "What is most worrisome to us is that the line that has traditionally separated the military from civilian policing is fading away." According to Lynch, "We see it as one of the most disturbing trends in the criminal justice area—the militarization of police tactics."[159]

Now the #Occupy movement and highly publicized official responses to it are forcing the public to confront what its police forces have become.

THE NATO PROTESTS: EXCESSIVE POLICING

I live only seven blocks from the conference center in Chicago where the North Atlantic Treaty Organization (NATO) meetings were held in May of 2012. What was disturbing about this event was the overwhelming number of police, dressed in heavy riot gear, who appeared days before the meeting. Literally dozens of helicopters roared overhead all the time, and streets were blocked with snowplows and heavy gates.

Yet the marches and speeches were largely peaceful, and even the confrontation with police after the end of the march on Sunday largely consisted of demonstrators linking arms and pushing at police, and police pushing back as

Demonstrator at NATO summit in Chicago.
Paul Weiskel, May 22, 2012

they tried to move the protestors away from the conference center. There was no looting and no cars set on fire, as has happened in European protests, for example. After observing the massively militarized police activity that descended on my neighborhood for days, the police presence seemed more provocative than preventive.

I also began to wonder if I was witnessing the new NATO in action. NATO (the North Atlantic Treaty Organization) is a strategic alliance of countries from North America and Europe who signed a mutual defense treaty on April 4, 1949, to defend themselves from possible aggression by the Soviet Union. It is a relic of the Cold War. What is NATO's mission in a post–Cold War world, when the biggest problem faced by both the European alliance and the United States is economic?

As European countries such as Greece have descended into economic chaos and protest austerity measures by taking to the streets, domestic control of citizen unrest may be NATO's next function. Change may also come at the ballot box, as happened in France and Greece. But for Europe, as well as for the United States, the economic picture is not bright, and millions, many of them young people, will continue to be out of work or underemployed. They will take to the streets, as they have already done.

British economist Shabir Razvi[160] warned in advance of this particular NATO meeting, and the meeting of the G8—the eight economic superpowers—that there is a prospect of uncontrollable civil unrest looming over European Union member states as a result of the economic austerity measures being implemented in EU countries. "We are living through a phase at this moment whereby the pressures on the ordinary people will ignite something, which the ruling elite may not be able to control," he noted. While President Obama called for job growth at the G8 meeting, fiscal responsibility (i.e., austerity measures) was also a theme. The pressures on ordinary people will certainly continue.

Thus, the NATO showcase in Chicago was actually less inside the McCormick Center, where the meetings were held, than outside, on the streets. NATO's future may very well be cooperation with police forces responsible for internal security in the NATO countries, as we enter the age of domestic unrest.

The world, not just NATO, is facing a stark choice. Will the new face of "peace" become pacification in the ever-increasing domestic militarization of police, and finally the merging of the military with police forces? Or will the future of actual peace be a jobs agenda that really does reverse the alarming trend of economic inequality, not only in the United States, but also around the world?

In the United States today, the militarization of the police and the use of excessive force in the face of largely nonviolent citizen demonstrations is a huge threat to democracy. From the time of the Roman occupation of Israel, regimes that have used violence against citizens who are simply demanding economic equality and human rights is a response of fear and weakness, not strength. That leads to tyranny. Strong democracies trust their citizens.

It is also a huge violation of the Christian faith to live silently with such militarized responses to efforts for societal change. When soldiers came to arrest Jesus in the Garden of Gethsemane, one of those with Jesus took out a sword and struck the slave of the high priest, cutting off his ear. "Put your sword back into its place," admonished Jesus, "for all who take the sword will perish by the sword" (Matthew 26:52).

It is not only swords. Tanks, machine guns, rubber bullets, tasers, tear gas, pepper spray, water canons, and sound canons are others ways we can perish unless we reverse this trend of relying on weaponry to solve the problems of our society.

We have the resources to become a more just and equitable society. What is needed is the will to accomplish this. Christians need to recognize that the path to a more decent society is to follow Jesus, and there is a biblical roadmap Christians can use to work alongside people of other faiths and humanist values to help create such a society. This biblical roadmap, found in the Gospels, shows Christians that where the hungry are fed, the sick are cared for, peace is made instead of war, and righteousness (justice) is desired above all else, Jesus is found.

9

#OccupytheApocalypse: Jesus and Economic Justice

Blessed are the poor in spirit, for theirs is the kingdom of heaven.

Blessed are those who mourn, for they will be comforted.

Blessed are the meek, for they will inherit the earth.

Blessed are those who hunger and thirst for righteousness, for they will be filled.

Blessed are the merciful, for they will receive mercy.

Blessed are the pure in heart, for they will see God.

Blessed are the peacemakers, for they will be called children of God.

Blessed are those who are persecuted for righteousness' sake, for theirs is the kingdom of heaven.

Blessed are you when people revile you and persecute you and utter all kinds of evil against you falsely on my account. Rejoice and be glad, for your reward is great in heaven, for in the same way they persecuted the prophets who were before you. (Matthew 5:3–11, *New Revised Standard Version*)

When the Son of Man comes in his glory, and all the angels with him, then he will sit on the throne of his glory. All the nations will be gathered before him, and he will separate people one from another as a shepherd separates the sheep from the goats, and he will put the sheep at his right hand and the goats at the left. Then the king will say to those at his right hand, 'Come, you that are blessed by my Father, inherit the kingdom prepared for you from the foundation of the world; for I was hungry and you gave me food, I was thirsty and you gave me something to drink, I was a stranger and you welcome me, I was naked and you gave me clothing, I was sick and you took care of me, I was in prison and you visited me.' Then the righteous will answer him, 'Lord, when was it that we saw you hungry and gave you food, or thirsty and gave you something to drink? And when was it that we saw you a stranger and welcome you, or naked and gave you clothing? And when was it that we saw you sick or in prison and visited you?' And the king will answer them, 'Truly I tell you, just as you did it to one of the least of these who are members of my family, you did it to me.' Then he will

> *say to those at his left hand, 'You that are accursed depart from me into the eternal fire prepared for the Devil and his angels; for I was hungry and you gave me no food, I was thirsty and you gave me nothing to drink, I was a stranger and you did not welcome me, naked and you did not give me clothing, sick and in prison and you did not visit me.' Then they also will answer, 'Lord, when was it that we saw you hungry or thirsty or a stranger or naked or sick or in prison and did not take care of you?' Then he will answer them, 'Truly I tell you, just as you did not do it to one of the least of these, you did not do it to me.' And these will go away into eternal punishment, but the righteous into eternal life.* (Matthew 25:31–46, *New Revised Standard Version*)

God did not send Jesus of Nazareth to suffer and die for our sins. Instead, Jesus came to teach and to show us, by example, how to treat each other, how to form community, and how to resist injustice with nonviolence and truth.

As I mentioned before, in Mel Gibson's *The Passion of the Christ*, Jesus' Sermon on the Mount lasts less than *40 seconds*, while Jesus is flogged, from beginning to end, for *40 minutes*. This warps and distorts the life *and* the death of Jesus. Jesus was tortured and killed not to fulfill some cosmic plan, but by order of the Roman occupying powers with the collaboration of the Temple elites. Jesus was tortured and killed precisely because of the kind of teaching he shared in the Sermon on the Mount, and because he put it into practice. Jesus was tortured and killed because he not only talked the talk of renewal of the Jewish people, connecting their spiritual rejuvenation to their practices on debt and economic justice, he walked the walk, and that is what threatened the Roman occupiers and split the Jewish community between the ordinary people and some of the Jewish elites, though of course, not all.

Jesus also taught that the real apocalypse, the eruption of God's reign of justice and mercy, is not a violent cataclysm at the end of history. Matthew's Gospel records a vision of the end-times judgment, the separation of the "sheep and the goats," that is, the saved and the damned, based on how people treat each other every day. Do you feed the hungry, clothe the naked, take care of the sick, and care about those in prison? Or do you just ignore the needy, and not even see them? But the teaching is more than just "be nice to each other." The teaching of Jesus states explicitly that when we feed, comfort, and care for each other, we are actually doing this *to Jesus*.

This teaching by Jesus in Matthew is a very different view of apocalypse than that presented in the Book of Revelation, especially as interpreted by conservative Christians predicting an imminent Rapture. This has entered popular culture through the *Left Behind* series of novels. The "good" Christians will be raptured and taken bodily into heaven, escaping the wrath to come.

The revelation to John of Patmos was, in the time of its composition, not about how all the good people will be saved before the final judgment as much as it was a virulent critique of Roman imperial power. But in truth, it is a vision of what will happen at the end of history, as the final trumpet sounds. It is not the judgment as presented by Jesus of Nazareth. According to Jesus, what we need to be concerned about is the *Apocalypse Now*. We need to #OccupytheApocalypse and take back its meaning for what is happening to us right here and now.

THE KINGDOM OF GOD PROGRAM OF JESUS OF NAZARETH

The members of the Jesus movement were known for eating and drinking together, taking care of the poor, and treating others with justice and mercy, including those who were considered sinners. The eating and drinking part is important, as is the radical hospitality of the Jesus movement. It embodies the presence of the Kingdom of God among the movement and shows it is a time for celebration.

Jesus, in fact, gets a little frustrated with all the criticism of John's movement and then his own. "For John the Baptist has come eating no bread and drinking no wine and you say, 'He has a demon'; the Human One has come eating and drinking, and you say, 'Look, a glutton and a drunkard, a friend of tax collectors and sinners!'" (Luke 7:33–34).[161] Jesus and his followers acted in a different way, living out the Kingdom of God in their midst through the kind of community they built, not just through their teaching.

One aspect of the #Occupy movement in 2011 was how much time the #OWS camps spent on just acting a different way. This way of living into another vision takes building community. This is why, in fact, #Occupy was so successful in 2011. The camps provided not just a way to create visibility for the movement, but a way to literally occupy a different reality, one that, like the Jesus movement, was about feeding, sharing, caring, and acting together. These were miniature societies, real communities designed to help people understand that power can be shared and that the corporate definition of human life is the real violence to our society. Dog-eat-dog capitalism pits us against each other instead of being a place where there is adequate food, shelter, work, and play for all.

The dismantling of the #Occupy camps, often with tremendous militarized police force as happened in Oakland, California, and other places, has fragmented the movement. As is noted in this book, the actions of #Occupy continue, especially in the opposition to foreclosures and the work of students on student debt. Occupiers are also working with unions to battle corporations to keep them from continuously cutting wages and benefits. The media is fond of predicting the demise of #Occupy,[162] though its action continues.

All real change takes a very long time, sometimes as long as a generation. It will take more than a year or two for Americans to recognize how and why their economic opportunities have diminished, and that without action at the grassroots, this economic decline will only worsen. Yet, we can see some change now as the #OWS movement has brought the terms the 1% and the 99% into mainstream American discourse. This is the beginning of a change in attitude toward wealth and poverty. #Occupy has given a name and an analysis to the epidemic of rising income inequality, and that insight is not going away any time soon.

#Occupy is a broad social movement for change, and it includes both secular and multi-faith perspectives. But it is not, and never will be, the Kingdom of God on earth. It can, however, be a sign to Christians that they should occupy their own scriptures on money and power in ways that institutional Christianity today fails to do, and that they should build strong communities that act in a different way than the

society around them. Currently, the charge against institutional Christianity is that it talks a good game, but doesn't really walk the walk.

THE KINGDOM OF GOD PROGRAM OF JESUS TODAY

The failure to put the teachings of Jesus of Nazareth into practice is a critique that has often been leveled at the institutional church throughout the history of Christianity. It has surfaced today in the views of the Millennial generation, those aged 18 to 29. This generation is far less involved with institutional religion than previous generations.[163] As the blog post "Hypocritical and Judgmental? Church maybe, Jesus never" on *millennialsthinktank*[164] shows, this age group tends to see the church as "hypocritical, sheltered, judgemental [sic]," and they do not see it as meeting their spiritual needs. Significant numbers of Millennials are "experiencing a disconnect between church and life," but they are also very determined to change the world.

But while Millennials may hate institutional religion, they love Jesus. The YouTube video "Why I Hate Religion, But Love Jesus"[165] went viral overnight. Jefferson Bethke, 22, posted his "poem against legalism, self-righteousness, self-justification and hypocrisy" of religious institutions, and his love for Jesus, on the web one evening. He made a bet with his roommates about how many hits it would get by morning. The highest guess was six thousand. It got one hundred thousand views overnight[166] and at last count was over 20 million.

The longing for integrity between the teachings of Jesus and the actions of Christians is part of this phenomenon, though, of course, not the whole. But if Christianity hopes to be relevant to the lives of the next generation, it needs to become the kind of living embodiment of the Kingdom of God that characterized the early Jesus movement.

Occupying scripture on money and power shows the way forward for a progressive Christianity faced with declining institutional relevance. But this way forward is fraught with challenge and difficulty, the same kind of difficulty faced by Jesus and his disciples as they tried to live out the reality of the Kingdom of God in their midst. It is well to keep in mind that walking the walk of the teachings of Jesus takes more than a YouTube video.

The movement to follow Jesus and live out the specifics of what he taught has never disappeared; it has continued to exist alongside institutional Christianity and has been made real over and over again in communal work for peace, justice, and economic equality. But it has never been easy.

THE COST OF DISCIPLESHIP

Dietrich Bonhoeffer, the famous German theologian and ethicist who was eventually hanged by the Nazis for resisting Hitler, came to believe that the teachings of Jesus, as exemplified in the Sermon on the Mount verses cited at the beginning of this chapter, were to be taken literally. He learned that from the African American church and its involvement in the struggle for racial justice in America.

This was a direct challenge to what was happening in Germany in the 1930s as the Christian church came more and more under the influence of the Nazis and their consolidation of power. It eventually led to the establishment of a *Reichskirche* (German Church), created to promote the state religion. These German Christians interpreted all Jesus' teachings subjectively, convinced that a literal reading produced legalism. Instead, in their view, a believer could develop certain internal attitudes by reading the New Testament and still outwardly obey the Third Reich. Thus, their subjective view of what Jesus taught enabled them to put love of country first and see Hitler and the Third Reich's rise to power as God's purpose revealed through scripture.

Bonhoeffer encountered the African American church in 1930, when he came to Union Theological Seminary in New York City as a post-doctoral Fellow. He met Frank Fisher, an African American and fellow seminarian who introduced him to the Abyssinian Baptist Church and the African American church experience. Bonhoeffer heard Adam Clayton Powell, Sr. preach the Gospel of Social Justice as lived in the struggles of the African American experience. He discovered in the black church that the whole church had to literally live Christian fellowship in action. Bonhoeffer began to understand the deep consequences of racism in the African American experience and to translate this into the anti-Semitism being generated with such virulence in Germany.[167]

In 1931, Bonhoeffer returned to Germany and was faced with the rise of a state religion along with the rule of the Third Reich. In 1934, a group calling itself the Confessing Church broke away from the German Christian church. They affirmed the relevance of scripture to modern life, indeed, to what was happening in Germany. In 1937, Bonhoeffer published *The Cost of Discipleship*, a call to his fellow German Christians to follow the teachings of Jesus on discipleship more literally, especially as seen in the Sermon on the Mount, and to the apply these teachings to their witness in the world. The Bible, Bonhoeffer asserts, is not an abstraction.[168]

But in claiming that we need to follow the teachings of Jesus in this world, Bonhoeffer acknowledges this is a costly decision. We can't just claim that Christ "paid the price" for our sins and go along our merry way, conforming to the injustices of this world. This is what Bonhoeffer calls "cheap grace." Cheap grace means "the justification of the sin without justification of the sinner." Cheap grace denies discipleship. Bonhoeffer defines discipleship as "our becoming like Christ who enables us to model our lives on his as the only 'Pattern' we must follow."

The Sermon on the Mount is the centerpiece of Jesus' teaching, according to Bonhoeffer. Bonhoeffer ultimately joined the resistance against Hitler's Germany. He was imprisoned and finally hanged by the Nazis.

But rather than follow the teachings of Jesus that we need to take care of each other here and now, creating community and resisting oppression, many Christians have decided that they don't need to worry about all that because history is about to come to a violent end, where the faithful will be Raptured and the rest condemned.

#OCCUPYTHEAPOCALYPSE

In 1995, Tim LaHaye and Jerry B. Jenkins published *Left Behind: A Novel of the Earth's Last Days.* This was the first in a series of extremely popular novels on the Rapture. The "Rapture" refers to the idea that true Christian believers will be "caught up" into heaven right before the violent judgment that will occur at the Second Coming of Christ. The rest of humanity, the sinners and unbelievers, will be left behind to suffer the pangs of judgment for a thousand years. A staggering

41 percent of Americans, according to a 2010 Pew poll, believe that Christ will or probably will return in their lifetimes.[169]

But what happens to our faith when our eyes are focused on the imminent end of history, and not on the hungry, the sick, the poor, and those in prison who are right in front of us, right now? What happens is we miss the very core of what Jesus taught, and we are unable even to understand that the real Apocalypse is happening this minute, in history.

The real Apocalypse is economic; those who are "left behind" are left behind in this economy, not in some fantastical Rapture. And it is fantastical. Every single prediction that Christ is about to return, such as the predictions of Harold Camping in 2011, has been proved wrong.

But the economic Apocalypse is upon us. This Apocalypse is the accumulation of calamitous economic decisions the United States has made over the past thirty years or more, but particularly during the previous administration, which have set this country on a course toward great devastation. "Great devastation" is one of the definitions of the term Apocalypse. This devastation is being caused by the biblical image of four horsemen, only these four horsemen are called war, recession, tax cuts, and debt.

Two unfunded wars and tax cuts for the rich have created the national debt apocalypse. The Iraq War is the "three trillion dollar war" according to Joseph Stiglitz, Nobel laureate and economist.[170] The Bush administration, after "wildly lowballing" the cost of the Iraq war at 50 to 60 billion dollars, continued to conceal the real bottom line, according to Stiglitz. Along with the expensive war in Afghanistan that is still going on, these two wars together are the fiscal iceberg that hit the U.S. deficit with calamitous results.

Another cause of the current debt Apocalypse is the Bush-era tax cuts. Unless these tax cuts are repealed, they will be the death of the United States as a decent, jobs-producing economy over the long term. These tax cuts are a major cause of the explosion in the deficit. But the economic proposals from conservatives, including Paul Ryan and Mitt Romney, will instead make massive cuts to social programs that care for the poor, the elderly, children, and those seeking work.

The meaning of *revelation* is to uncover what is hidden. What is hidden inside conservative budget proposals is the end of the social safety net for many Americans. We would return to the American of before the mid-twentieth century, where the elderly sometimes starved, children were often malnourished, many went without even a minimum of healthcare, and those who were out of work were out of luck. If the conservative budget proposals take effect, the non-partisan Center on Budget and Policy Priorities estimates, by 2022, non-defense spending would be cut by 59 percent, including programs like Medicare and Medicaid.[171]

LIVING THE SERMON ON THE MOUNT

Jesus' teaching in the Sermon on the Mount is at the centerpiece of his ministry, but without understanding the whole of his movement, the sermon is easy to misunderstand. Some in the history of Christianity have internalized its message like the German Christians did and thus lost (or deliberately ignored) the powerful public witness that is central to what Jesus meant. Protestant liberals can get distracted by questions of "did Jesus really say this, or do that?" and lose sight of the need to not only follow the teaching, but also act it out

The author, on the mountain overlooking the Sea of Galilee in Israel, teaching seminary students about the Sermon on the Mount.

Jami Huisjen-Scott, January 2011

in a public way, in opposition to political forces that tempt us to put the worship of money and power ahead of taking care of the neighbor. And conservatives want to focus on the fact that the whole historical human project is coming to an end anyway, so why try to effect justice here and now?

Justice here and now was central not only to the Sermon on the Mount, but also to the Jesus movement, and it needs to be public, not just private. Christians must resist any budget proposals that would put the burden of balancing the budget on the elderly, the poor, children, and those who are sick and out of work. We need a positive moral case for government in a democracy as an extension of Jesus' teaching on caring for one another. In a democracy, government is of the people, by the people, and for the people.

It's US, all of us, and the way we take care of each other. We have a moral responsibility to our fellow citizens, both from a civil and a moral perspective. We are one people. The problem is that some of us—in fact, many of us—are struggling in this difficult economy, and we need to help those folks out. Government is supposed to do that.

An individualistic reading of the Sermon on the Mount might lead you to conclude that we don't need government programs to help our neighbors in need; churches can do that. Rev. Joel Hunter, a prominent Evangelical, has pointed out how unrealistic that view can be.[172] Hunter's church does a huge amount of humanitarian work, but, he says, they can't do it all without the government: "Look at the math. It is ridiculous to even, just look at the SNAP—Supplemental Nutrition Assistance Program, the old Food Stamps program—it has been estimated by . . . the Center on Budget and Policy Priorities that the average church in America would literally have to double its budget and just take that extra budget and give to hungry people. And that is just one government program. So let's not fool ourselves."

We are totally fooling ourselves if we think we can have a decent society when the rich don't pay their fair share of taxes and the budget is balanced on the backs of the poor. Jesus' famous line on paying taxes is "Render to Caesar the things that are Caesar's, and to God the things that are God's" (Mark 12:17, *King James Version*). What is less well remembered is the reason Jesus called out both the political and the religious leaders who asked him whether you should pay your taxes: Jesus "knew their hypocrisy" (Mark 12:15).

What is hypocrisy but fooling yourself? That's what Jesus is talking about. Don't be a hypocrite. Take the teachings of the Sermon on the Mount seriously, not only as how you want to live as a Christian yourself, giving generously and serving those in need, but demanding that in a democratic society this is how we need to treat each other.

The Kingdom of God is a vision of the reality of justice and peace that Christians should pursue now, not wait until a violent Rapture occurs. As citizens in a democracy, Christians, other people of faith, and people of humanist values are called to contribute to the vision of the whole and make the best case they can for our national economic values.

Christians bring the Jesus movement to this effort, knowing that Jesus' words and deeds matched and that we are called to resist hypocrisy and to have integrity in our faithful witness on what we do with money and power.

10

Conclusion: Can the Church #Occupy?

THE #OCCUPY MOVEMENT ITSELF IS NOT THE CHURCH, NOR should the church try to claim that it could become the new face of #Occupy. But the #Occupy movement is a sign to the church, in the religious meaning of "sign" as message from God. It is, as are all religious "signs," not exactly given in the form of dictation, but this movement means something profound for our times in a religious sense.

Here are some ways #Occupy is a sign:

THE BIBLICAL TEACHINGS OF JESUS ARE REAL

Money is real, and so is the temptation to be greedy. Power is real, and so is the temptation to abuse it. This is the meaning of what Jesus really taught and did, and it is the biblical message Christians need to occupy today.

Progressive Christians rarely talk about money and power in the way they interpret the Bible. Instead, they have studied biblical interpretation based on archeological evidence, language study, and historical materials to better understand the composition of the biblical texts.

The problem is that while biblical interpretation is important to understand the origins of the scriptures, the interpretation can become an end in itself. This has hampered the prophetic biblical voice of progressive Christians. Progressive Christians need to recognize that the point of reading the Bible is to gain insight on how to live out the teaching today in ways that make human sense. And progressive Christians need to grasp what's real about what the Bible teaches, especially on money and power. Nothing, absolutely nothing, is more real in human life than greed and the abuse of power.

The Christian Right in this country has claimed the Bible as their warrant for a politically conservative agenda that would deny equal rights to lesbian, gay, bisexual, and transgender citizens; keep women from exercising reproductive responsibility; defend torture, deny climate change, support the endless production of war and domestic surveillance; and roll back regulation of our economic institutions in the name of God and "freedom." None of these are biblically based values.

There are Evangelical Christians, however, who have a biblically based theology that leads them to a different perspective on what discipleship requires in terms of their witness in the world on justice and peace. Leading Evangelicals have released a wide-ranging book about how Evangelicals can be "right-wing Christians and left-wing voters." This work, *A New Evangelical Manifesto: A Kingdom Vision for the Common Good,*[173] edited by David Gushee, makes this point comprehensively. As the book documents, "There is a significant, emerging segment of conservatively theological Christians who agree with politically liberal counterparts while staying true to their own faith regarding a wide variety of political issues in contemporary America."[174]

Catholics too exhibit much greater diversity in how they relate their church teachings, the scriptures and their witness in the world than one would realize from listening only to the pronouncements of the Vatican or the American Catholic Bishops. Catholics in Alliance for the Common Good,[175] as well as Network,[176] a Catholic social justice lobby, discussed below, are strong examples of this. These Catholics have a strong tradition of Catholic social teaching on which they are basing their witness for social justice and the common good today. From Father John Ryan, who, as was discussed earlier, helped make the moral case for the New Deal in the early part of the twentieth century, to Pope John Paul II in his encyclical on work and human dignity, to the National Council of Catholic Bishops pastoral letter on peace,[177] Catholic teaching provides a wealth of insight on which these current Catholics are drawing.

All Christians, left, right, and center, as well as Unitarians, can come together around the simple truth that the biblical message as taught by Jesus of Nazareth was the love of God and neighbor acted out in the Jesus movement. What Jesus and his followers did was build up communities of equality and mutual support, economic fairness, gender equality, and live a life of celebration of one another and our love of God. And where these values were not realized in his society, Jesus and his followers protested. That's real, and that should be the message that the church not only teaches, but also lives.

BRING TENT

God is not to be found in a concrete and glass sanctuary or painted into stained glass. God is found on the move, occupying a tent as slaves escape, with Jesus on dusty roads in the Galilee or the stone streets of Jerusalem, and with gatherings of people protesting civil rights abuse, war, and the impoverishment of the many to enrich the few.

God is a movement God, and unless we as Christians quit mistaking our institutional forms of faith for the movement of God in history, we won't be able to see the signs even if they are written in letters a thousand feet high. "When did we see you, Lord?" Jesus is asked. But Jesus was right in front of them in the poor, the sick, and the imprisoned, and they never saw him. The trick is to actually "see," and you can't see what's happening if you don't get out of your house and out of your church and move around where people are gathering in the streets.

Yet, signs are imperfect, and human movements for peace and justice are imperfect. They are not synonymous with the Kingdom of God. The Kingdom of God is only glimpsed in these movements.

It is a mystery that in some of the most titanic struggles for simple human dignity, God seems to be absent. God moves, but will be who God will be (Exodus 3). Any effort to control God, to bend God to fit a movement, is, by definition, idolatry. Indeed, as Anne Lamott puts it so well, "You can safely assume that you've created God in your own image when it turns out that God hates all the same people you do."[178]

Faith and the struggles for a better society are related, but they are never identical.

But if some movements have tended to mistake God for their own image, this idolatry has been committed a thousand-fold by the institutional churches. This indeed is the great weakness of institutionalized religion: it tries to make its institutions synonymous with a tent-dwelling God. It never works.

Recently, we have seen this attempt to control God played out as idolatry in the suppressive tactics of the Vatican against its own U.S. nuns.[179] But these actions by the Catholic hierarchy in turn inspired a local Catholic pastor to write a biblical denunciation of the Vatican in the parish bulletin of Blessed Trinity Catholic Church in Cleveland under the simple headline "From the Desk of Fr. Doug."

This pastor powerfully makes the argument I have tried to make in this book about what the Bible really says. The following is only part of what Fr. Doug had to say:

> *The Vatican sounded like the Pharisees of the New Testament;—legalistic, paternalistic and orthodox—while "the good sisters" were the ones who were feeding the hungry, clothing the naked, visiting the sick and imprisoned, educating the immigrant.*[180]

Fr. Doug is right that the Vatican is all about control; it is about substituting its own power for the power of God for good in this world. And that is hypocrisy.

Rather than be silenced by the Vatican, in the summer of 2012 these nuns rented a bus[181] and traveled around the United States witnessing the priorities for people of faith to take care of the poor and protesting cuts in federal programs that help the poor and working families. They have particularly targeted the federal budget that was passed by the House of Representatives and proposed by Representative Paul D. Ryan, the Wisconsin Republican who cited his Catholic faith to justify the cuts.

"We're doing this because these are life issues," said Sister Simone Campbell, executive director of Network,[182] the organization of Catholic sisters particularly targeted by the Vatican. "And by lifting up the work of Catholic sisters, we will demonstrate the very programs and services that will be decimated by the House budget."[183]

The nuns' bus is a version of the "tent" that captures the moveable presence of God in the midst of struggles for justice and peace.

QUIT THE HYPOCRISY

Young Americans today distrust the institutional church partly because the church is so hypocritical. It talks a good game, but when it comes down to really dealing with the issues of extremes of wealth and poverty, lack of healthcare, privatization of prisons, and the use of violence in war and social control—all the issues Jesus said his ministry was about—the churches are often missing in action.

Either they are preoccupied with a personal spirituality that may give to charity but does not challenge social injustices, or they are willing to witness about injustice but neglect to deal with the deepest issues of money and power.

The conflict between institutional religion and the aims of #OWS can clearly be seen in the case of Trinity Church in New York City and the #Occupy protestors.[184] Seven protestors, among them a retired Episcopal bishop, George

Packard, and a Harlem priest, were arrested and subsequently convicted of trespassing on Trinity Church's property. Protestors had wanted to use part of the church-owned property for a winter encampment. The sentences were limited in most cases to community service, but many felt the church had acted to protect its corporate investments rather than allow protestors to use church-owned property for a winter camp.

Bishop Packard said he was surprised, disappointed, and saddened by the trial's outcome. "Trinity did not have to pursue the charges, but it opted to 'protect fiduciary interests,'" he told Episcopal News Service. "It's pretty sad. I mean, this is what our church has come to. You don't have enough pledging units to sustain many places. So we depend on the cash flow of corporate investment. It's a caricature of what the Gospel is."[185] Trinity Wall Street, founded in 1697, has become a major commercial real estate owner in lower Manhattan through its holdings in lower Manhattan.[186]

The Occupiers, young and old, see this as the face of the church, captive to corporate interests and unable to really side with the poor.

Some churches and religious organizations, however, do walk the walk and not just talk the talk. They are putting the words of Jesus together with their actions. For example, Judson Memorial Church, along with other ministers and laypeople, created a golden calf, the idol worshipped in Exodus 32 that Moses condemns, and brought it to Wall Street. In the words of Rev. Jennifer Butler, a Presbyterian minister, she and the others brought the calf and marched with it "to reflect on the condemnation of greed throughout Scripture. The calf was displayed in the sanctuary during worship and carried at the front of our procession through Lower Manhattan. In

A golden calf is featured in an Occupy Wall Street demonstration.

Erik McGregor, October 9, 2011

church and in the streets, the cheers and prayers were overwhelming. Photographers and TV crews flocked to us. Apparently you don't need to know your Exodus to understand a symbol of idolatry."[187]

But what was, or even more importantly, is the kind of Christian community formed at Judson Memorial Church? This church and many others like it around the country strive to actually form communities inside the sanctuary that can serve as the kind of alternative community the #Occupy camps aspired to be. When the golden calf arrived at the church, Rev. Schaper had it placed in the sanctuary.

"We were moved to pray, which I have to admit is not something we do that often on Saturday nights. We took turns reading Exodus 32 verse by verse."[188]

Spiritual formation that integrates the text, the worship practice, and the witness in the world is what the church needs to be doing today.

THE CHURCH IS NOT JUST THE CHURCH ANYMORE

The traditional church structures of Protestant denominations, the American Catholic Church, and other religious faiths are no longer necessarily how people find community in faith, nor are they silos of religious identity. Catholics, Presbyterians, United Church of Christ members, Unitarian Universalists, or Protestant Evangelicals who recognize that we need to walk the walk of the Sermon on the Mount as Jesus taught are making common cause on issues of economic justice and fairness and are far more likely to find themselves shoulder to shoulder with one another than with other members of their individual churches. These alliances shift and re-form, but a fairly reliable coalition has been built among those who share these commitments.

Thus, churches themselves are not necessarily the places where people of faith find their needs for community and meaning met and their communities of solidarity for action for justice in the world. There is a shift in what we think of as "church" that is starting to include organizations and networks of what we could call "para-church" movements. Some of these movements are, at times, interfaith and interreligious, bringing those of different faiths together in coalitions that are more than political organizations.

There are many examples of this around the country, and in fact the emergence of the #Occupy movement was instrumental in calling out those who want something more from religious community today than they are getting from their own institutions. For example, in the Los Angeles area, the #Occupy movement at first seemed a "puzzling challenge" to faith leaders, then as a "real center of focused attention and energy, and then finally as a still-resonant avatar for how we focus our work forward," according to the Reverend Peter Laarman, Executive Director of Progressive Christians Uniting.

These faith leaders in the LA area simply accepted the #Occupy encampments and the General Assembly process on their own terms and demonstrated solidarity by setting up an Interfaith Sanctuary tent. According to Laarman, these faith leaders "were simply grateful that the core issues of economic and social justice had been made dramatically visible in the public square (literally)." Some of these faith leaders translated the message into their own church worship spaces.[189]

Laarman also uses the language of sign to describe Occupy LA. "The real power of Occupy LA as a sign to area faith leaders was revealed at the point at which LA's mayor, frustrated with negotiations to re-locate the Occupation, announced that the encampment would soon be removed. Several *hundred* faith leaders—far more than just the 'usual suspects' progressive fringe—signed an appeal letter to the mayor and police chief urging them to find alternatives to forced removal. Faith leaders also organized an in-person meeting with the mayor and chief just prior to the eviction, demanding a nonviolent process and insisting on being involved as designated observers. For the interfaith leaders at the core of Interfaith Sanctuary in Los Angeles, the entire experience both branded us and brought us together as no previous interaction had done."

And the group that came together through that experience has not disbanded.[190]

The Interfaith aspect of this response is part of the realignment of faith in our time. The Reverend James Forbes has described our time as experiencing an "interfaith Great Awakening" that has the potential to bring about both spiritual renewal and social transformation, precisely because our times are so unsettled. Our troubled and disconcerting era is exactly the kind of time in which previous awakenings occurred in American history. "In each of the great awakenings there has been a perceived sense of out of balance, out of kilter, insecurity, change beyond our capacity to cope. I think we are a prime suspect for a great awakening because we surely meet that requirement. Out of kilter, broken down, scared, not able to even believe our ideals are feasible."[191]

Surely Rev. Forbes is right. Our times are so unstable, even brittle, there's a good chance something new can break through the cracks.

Diana Butler Bass builds on Forbes' point but adds this absolutely crucial instruction: "Show up for the awakening."[192]

Praying is good, even essential, but you have to act and act together with others in community. This is the Jesus movement in a nutshell.

TWEET IT

Cyberspace and the advent of social media has given us another way to build community. Rev. Meg Riley, a Unitarian Universalist minister, has run online worship services for about a year, gathering several hundred people weekly on a livestream channel.[193]

Riley comments:

The center of the action is people's direct connection with one another, which we then support through Facebook and Google+ small groups, listserves, and direct contact with ministers. It is amazing how much open source technology supports nonhierarchical, creative, participatory community. Next year we will try a face-to-face opportunity to do a service trip; we'll be curious to see if the online community can bridge into something face-to-face. But the intimacy and support we develop together online are profound . . . Since I am not bound to the pulpit for my sermons, I am free to film wherever I experience the holy. Before my local Occupy movement was shut down, I filmed one homily there. I have filmed at Planned Parenthood and at my local dog park (talking about 'off leash faith')."

Rev. Riley is not waiting to figure out the answer to the question of whether the connections and relationships we make online are real. She and those who are worshipping in this way find their online community to be the "real deal" when it comes to building spiritual communities for social transformation in our time.

In short, yes, it is as real as the connection you feel to those with whom you are connecting in cyberspace. It is another way new spiritual communities are forming and reforming.

Our capacity to occupy our own lives and make them more meaningful, just, and sustainable is immeasurably increased by the advent of the age of the Internet. Just remember that the forces of destruction and demonization also have these tools and are using them to disrupt alternative communities to get as much money as they can and gain the power to control others. The Internet, as I have written, is in every way a mirror of the struggle of good and evil in our time.[194]

It is also crucial to remember that bodies are fed, sheltered, and cared for with love and justice in the physical world. Our cyber realities can contribute to that, but the touchstone for knowing Jesus in this world always comes back to the physical body. It is, as Gustavo Gutierrez taught, always a "matter of the stomach."

GET STARTED

I am proposing that you and I take a new faith journey, a journey into the Bible that may be totally unfamiliar to you. It has been unfamiliar to me, too. I did not learn this way of reading the Bible and seeing the world through the eyes of a street-level scripture primarily in my church or in seminary. I learned it from battered women, from Dr. Martin Luther King, Jr., from the Social Gospel pioneers of the early twentieth century, and from the #Occupy participants in the twenty-first century.

For some of you reading this book, what I am proposing will not be completely new, but for others this way of engaging the economic challenges of our times with the Bible as your guide will be very new and very challenging.

Don't worry. It is possible to get started wherever you are on this journey so far.

Get a New Revised Standard Version of the Bible and Read It

Go get an NRSV and start reading, using this book as your guide. Look up the passage or passages that I use at the beginning of each chapter in the book of the Bible where they are found. Read the verses before and after, thinking about the passage of scripture and where it is located in the Bible. Some texts are found in several different places, and the wording can be different. Ask yourself what difference you think that makes.

Once you've done that initial exploration, read the whole Gospel of Mark and eventually work your way through the whole New Testament. Then read the biblical prophets, starting with Isaiah, as that sacred text was so important to Jesus of Nazareth. Ultimately, read the whole Bible cover to cover.

Get Out on Your Own Streets

Walk or even drive through the neighborhoods of your town or city where there are the most foreclosures. Look in the paper and find a sheriff's sale of a foreclosed property. Go to the auction and merely observe.

If there is a college or university campus near you, visit the coffee shop and perhaps engage students there in discussions of their student debt. If you are a student yourself and overloaded with debt, try to find ways to tell people in your faith community about your struggles. Write a short piece for your faith community's national website, and be sure to copy your local congregation. If you do not have a congregation or don't know how to get your story out, write it up and send it to me at Chicago Theological Seminary (you can find me on the seminary website) and I will find a way to get your voice heard on the Internet. (Be sure to include permission to post your writing!)

Make an appointment with a loan officer at your local bank. Ask that person (politely of course) what their bank is doing to help with the mortgage crisis.

Visit a city council meeting and see what is being discussed.

Look at your town or city with new biblical eyes. What is actually happening?

Use Social Media

Almost everyone these days can find access to a computer, if not at home then at the public library, and many of us now have social media access on our phones. Get a Twitter account (Google how to do that and follow the instructions) and follow me on Twitter. I always tweet a #OccupytheBible verse, and you will get access to that. Follow the hashtag #OWS, and search #Occupy. Follow as many as you can and read the thread every day.

Begin to engage the issues in this book as you explore the resources of new media. Find stories of the economic struggles of ordinary Americans and post those links to others. Let people know your own story (but take care not to publicly share personal contact details on the Internet). The story is what matters.

As you get to know the #Occupy events in your area, support those you feel are important however you can. Go to events and simply engage people in conversation. If you are an #Occupy leader yourself, visit Christian religious leaders and tell them how you are rereading the Bible with new eyes as you have been active in the #Occupy movement.

Make the Connections

After you attend a sheriff's sale or drive through a neighborhood with a lot of foreclosures, come back to the Bible and reread the Parable of the Talents, for example. The way to #OccupytheBible is through a journey of insight and action, a circle where each activity helps you read the Bible with ever-new eyes, and each text challenges you to engage the world in a different way. Try to find a diverse group of people with whom to think, act, pray, and read so you can challenge each other.

Put your beliefs into political practice. Support candidates you feel will try to implement policies that will bring greater economic fairness, transparency, and accountability to our society. Volunteer to register people to vote. Make sure you vote.

Pray for your community and your country and your world.

Remember your goal is not to become a Bible scholar or a politician, but to become a more decent human being, helping to bring about the Kingdom of God here and now. And at the end of the day, remember that the Bible is a witness to that goal, but it is not the goal itself.

JESUS IS NOT IN THE TEXT, HE'S RIGHT IN FRONT OF YOU

One of the most powerful Easter sermons I ever heard was by The Reverend John Buchanan at Fourth Presbyterian Church in Chicago. Rev. Buchanan was reflecting on one of the early manuscripts of the Gospel of Mark that ends in the middle of a sentence. Scholars have always assumed that somehow the scribe was interrupted, though since the manuscript survived there would have been plenty of time to finish it after the interruption. It doesn't seem to make sense.

What Rev. Buchanan suggested is that what the half-finished sentence really means is that "Jesus is gone. He's not here in this text."

And when you #OccupytheBible you learn the same thing: Jesus isn't actually in the text, he's right in front of you and he wants you to follow him.

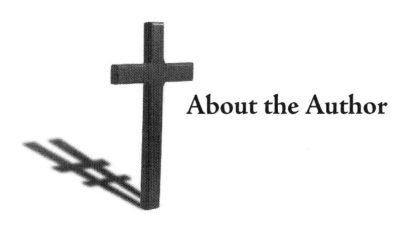

About the Author

Photo by Winnie Stackelberg.

REV. DR. SUSAN BROOKS THISTLEthwaite is a Professor of Theology at the Chicago Theological Seminary, and served as its president from 1998 to 2008. An ordained minister of the United Church of Christ since 1974, she's authored numerous books and has worked on two different translations of the Bible. She also writes a weekly column for the *Washington Post* (*On Faith*) and is a frequent media commentator on religion and public events.

Dr. Thistlethwaite currently serves on the boards of the Center for American Progress, and the Interfaith Youth Core. She received her PhD from Duke University, her Masters of Divinity (*summa cum laude*) from Duke Divinity School, and her B.A. from Smith College.

She lives and works in Chicago, Illinois.

Previous Publications

Metaphors for the Contemporary Church (1983)

A Just Peace Church, ed. (1986)

Lift Every Voice: Constructing Christian Theologies from the Underside, ed. with Mary Potter Engel (first edition, 1990)

Sex, Race, and God: Christian Feminism in Black and White (1991)

Casting Stones: Prostitution and Liberation in Asia and the United States, with Rita Nakashima Brock (1996)

The Inclusive Language Lectionary, Years A, B, and C, The National Council of Churches Inclusive Lectionary Committee (1987, originally published 1983–1985)

The New Testament and Psalms: An Inclusive Version, with the Inclusive Language Translation Committee (1995)

Adam, Eve, and the Genome: The Human Genome Project and Theology, ed. (2003)

Dreaming of Eden: American Religion and Politics in a Wired World (2010)

Interfaith Just Peacemaking: Jewish, Christian, and Muslim Perspectives on the New Paradigm of Peace and War (2012)

Endnotes

[1] Beverly Harrison, "The Power of Anger in the Work of Love," *Making the Connections: Essays in Feminist Social Ethics*, ed. Carol Robb (Boston: Beacon Press, 1985), p. 14.

[2] Mattathais Schwartz,"Pre-Occupied: The Origins and Future of Occupy Wall Street," *The New Yorker*, November 28, 2011, www.newyorker.com/reporting/2011/11/28/111128fa_fact_schwartz?currentPage=all.

[3] Adbusters, "Anonymous Joins #OCCUPYWALLSTREET," | Adbusters Culturejammer Headquarters,"*Adbusters*, August 23, 2011, www.adbusters.org/blogs/adbusters-blog/anonymous-joins-occupywallstreet.html.

[4] Ben Berkowitz, "From a Single Hashtag, a Protest Circled the World," Brisbane Times, October 11, 2011, www.brisbanetimes.com.au/technology/technology-news/from-a-single-hashtag-a-protest-circled-the-world-20111019-1m72j.html.

[5] Associated Press, "Judge Rules Against Occupy Wall Street Encampment," *First Amendment Center,* November 15, 2011, www.firstamendmentcenter.org/judge-rules-against-occupy-wall-street-encampment.

[6] Sidney Earl Mead, *The Nation with the Soul of a Church* (Macon, GA: Mercer University Press, 1985).

[7] Kyle Mantyle, "Jacobs: OWS Protests Driven by 'A Power of Darkness,'" *Right Wing Watch*, October 20, 2011, www.rightwingwatch.org/content/jacobs-ows-protests-driven-power-darkness.

[8] John Dominic Crossan, *God and Empire: Jesus Against Rome Then and Now* (San Francisco: HarperSanFrancisco, 2007), p. 122.

[9] *Frontline*, "Primary Sources: The Gospel Of Mary," *From Jesus to Christ*, FRONTLINE, PBS, April 1998.

[10] Christopher Ketchum, "The New Populists," *The American Prospect*, December 21, 2011, http://prospect.org/article/new-populists-0?utm_source=Daily+Digest&utm_campaign=b9a370b932-DD_12_13_1112_13_2011&utm_medium=email.

[11] Ben Popken, "Signs In Chicago Board of Trade Windows Say 'We Are The 1%,'" *The Consumerist*, October 6, 2011, http://consumerist.com/2011/10/signs-in-chicago-board-of-trade-windows-say-we-are-the-1.html.

[12] Susan Brooks Thistlethwaite, "Liberation Theology for Beginners," On Faith Panelists Blog, *The Washington Post*, August 30, 2010, http://newsweek.washingtonpost.com/onfaith/panelists/susan_brooks_thistle thwaite/2010/08/liberation_theology_for_beginners.html.

[13] *CBS News*, "Census Bureau Data: Half of U.S. Poor or Low Income," *CBS News*, December 15, 2011, www.cbsnews.com/8301-201_162-57343397/census-data-half-of-u.s-poor-or-low-income/.

[14] Daisy Grewal, "How Wealth Reduces Compassion," *Scientific American*, April 10, 2012, www.scientificamerican.com/article.cfm?id=how-wealth-reduces-compassion.

[15] Originally published by HarperSanFrancisco, 1990; published in a new and expanded edition by Orbis Press, 1998.

[16] Congressional Budget Office,"Trends in the Distribution of Household Income Between 1979 and 2007," *Congressional Budget Office*, October 25, 2011, http://cbo.gov/publication/42729.

[17] Congregation for the Doctrine of the Faith, "Instruction on Certain Aspects of the 'Theology of Liberation,'" *The Vatican*, August 6, 1984, www.vatican.va/roman_curia/congregations/cfaith/documents/rc_con_cfaith_doc_19840806_theology-liberation_en.html.

[18] Fr. Tony Lalli, "Dom Helder Camara: Poet, Mystic, Missionary," *Xavier Missionaries*, September 1, 1999, www.xaviermissionaries.org/M_Life/NL_Archives/99-N_Lett/BR_Helder_Camara.htm.

[19] Summit Ministries, "Liberation Theologians," *YouTube*, August 24, 2009, www.youtube.com/watch?v=bj81NtBDETI.

[20] James Martin, S.J., "Glenn Beck and Liberation Theology," *America Magazine,* August 29, 2010, www.americamagazine.org/blog/entry.cfm?entry_id=3224.

[21] Susan Brooks Thistlethwaite, "Glenn Beck's Worst Nightmare: The Early Church Was Socialist," *Washington Post*, April 14, 2010, http://onfaith.washingtonpost.com/onfaith/panelists/susan_brooks_thistlethwaite/2010/04/glenn_becks_worst_nightmare--the_early_church_was_socialist.html.

[22] Jim Wallis, *Rediscovering Values on Wall Street, Main Street, and Your Street* (New York: Simon and Schuster, 2010).

[23] Jay W. Richards, *Money, Greed, and God: Why Capitalism Is the Solution, Not the Problem* (New York: HarperCollins, 2010).

[24] Susan Brooks Thistlethwaite, "The Bible and Battered Women," *Christianity and Crisis* 41 (17): 309.

[25] Susan Brooks Thistlethwaite, "Be Suspicious of Religious Authorities Telling You What the Bible Says," On Faith Panelists Blog, *The Washington Post*, February 18, 2009, http://newsweek.washingtonpost.com/onfaith/panelists/susan_brooks_thistlethwaite/2009/02/be_suspicious_of_religious_aut.html.

[26] Mary Paula Walsh, *Feminism and Christian Tradition: An Annotated Bibliography and Critical Introduction to the Literature* (ABC-CLIO, May 30, 1999), http://books.google.com/books?id=ItaGeZfoSdgC&pg=PA386&lpg=PA386&dq=Thistlethwaite,+The+bible+and+Battered+women&source=bl&ots=2x5c_L0IR8&sig=CUIVv1KnOeasB0cgNzc0uvhsD6o&hl=en&sa=X&ei=XM8AT_feHMLoggfQ8bSjAg&ved=0CEAQ6AEwBg#v=onepage&q=Thistlethwaite%2C%20T&f=false.

[27] Cain Hope Felder, *Stony the Road We Trod: African American Biblical Interpretation* (Minneapolis, MN: Augsburg/Fortress, 1991).

[28] Robert James Scofield, "King's God: The Unknown Faith of Dr. Martin Luther King Jr.," *Tikkun Magazine,* www.tikkun.org/article.php/nov_dec_09_scofield.

[29] Ibid.

[30] The Rev. Dr. Martin Luther King, Jr., U.S. Constitution, "The I Have a Dream Speech," speech, Washington, D.C., August 28, 1963 *U.S. Constitution,* www.usconstitution.net/dream.html.

[31] The Rev. Dr. Martin Luther King, Jr., "Loving Your Enemies," sermon, Dexter Avenue Baptist Church, Montgomery, Alabama, November 17, 1957, *Write Spirit,* www.writespirit.net/inspirational_talks/political/martin_luther_king_talks/loving_your_enemies/.

[32] Ibid.

[33] Sheryl Gay Stolberg, "Shy U.S. Intellectual Created Playbook Used in a Revolution," *New York Times,* February 16, 2011, www.nytimes.com/2011/02/17/world/middleeast/17sharp.html?pagewanted=all.

[34] Stanford University, "Martin Luther King, Jr. and the Global Freedom Struggle," *Stanford University,* http://mlk-kpp01.stanford.edu/index.php/encyclopedia/encyclopedia/enc_martin_luther_king_jr_biography/.

[35] American Values Network, "Tea Party Jesus' 'Sermon on the Mall,'" The American Values *NetworkTea Party Jesus,* http://teapartyjesus.org/script-citations-2/.

[36] Lila Shapiro, "Occupy Wall Street's Librarians Make Demands at Rally," *Huffington Post,* November 23, 2011, www.huffingtonpost.com/2011/11/23/occupy-wall-street-library_n_1110950.html.

[37] Aaron B. Franzen, "Survey: Frequent Bible Reading Can Turn You Liberal," *Christianity Today,* October 12, 2011, www.christianitytoday.com/ct/2011/october/survey-bible-reading-liberal.html.

[38] Rachel Weiner, "Conservative Bible Project Cuts Out Liberal Passages," *Huffington Post,* March 18, 2010, www.huffingtonpost.com/2009/10/05/conservative-bible-projec_n_310037.html.

[39] Elaine Pagels, *The Origin of Satan* (New York: Random House, 1995), 49.

[40] See Upton Sinclair, *The Cry for Justice: An Anthology of the Literature of Social Protest*, pp. 247–8, www.archive.org/stream/cu31924032495883#page/n5/mode/2up.

[41] A. O. Scott, "*Bread and Roses* (2000) Film Review; On the Bumpy Road of a Union Drive," *New York Times*, June 1, 2001, http://movies.nytimes.com/movie/review?res=9B0CE7DE1E3CF932A35755C0A9679C8B63.

[42] Flavius Josephus, *The Wars of the Jews*, Book 5, Section 190, *Tufts University*, www.perseus.tufts.edu/hopper/text?doc=Perseus:text:1999.01.0148:book=5:section=190&highlight=magnificence%2Cnatural.

[43] Andrew Young, interview, *God in America* Episode Five: "The Soul of a Nation," www.pbs.org/godinamerica/view/.

[44] The historian and moralist, who was otherwise known simply as Lord Acton, expressed this opinion in a letter to Bishop Mandell Creighton in 1887: "Power tends to corrupt, and absolute power corrupts absolutely. Great men are almost always bad men."

[45] Jack Mirkinson, "Press Freedom Index: Occupy Wall Street Journalist Arrests Cost U.S. Dearly in Latest Survey," *Huffington Post*, January 25, 2012, www.huffingtonpost.com/2012/01/25/press-freedom-occupy-wall-street-us-arrests_n_1230825.html.

[46] *Against Heresies*, 5.1.1, in *Ante-Nicene Christianity Library*, vol. 9, ed. Alexander Roberts and James Donaldson (Edinburgh, Scotland: T. & T. Clark, 1869).

[47] Ibid., 5.21.2.

[48] Susan Brooks Thistlethwaite, "Can the 'Spirit of Tahrir Square' Survive in the Egyptian Transition to Democracy?" On Faith Panelists Blog, *The Washington Post*, June 10, 2011, www.washingtonpost.com/blogs/on-faith/post/can-the-spirit-of-tahrir-square-survive-in-the-egyptian-transition-to-democracy/2011/06/10/AGV1AkOH_blog.html.

[49] James Dunn, *Jews and Christians: The Parting of the Ways* (Grand Rapids, MI: Wm. B. Eerdmans, 1999), orig. published 1992, J. C. B. Mohr, p. 44.

[50] Josephus, *Antiquities of the Jews*, 17:213–4.

[51] Ched Myers, *Binding the Strong Man: A Political Reading of Mark's Story of Jesus* (Maryknoll, NY: Orbis Books, 1988, 2008), 301.

[52] Ibid., 300.

[53] Susan Brooks Thistlethwaite, *Dreaming of Eden: American Religion and Politics in a Wired World* (New York: Palgrave Macmillan, 2010), Chapter 4, "Financial Meltdown."

[54] Ibid.

[55] *Daily Beast*. "Keeping Economics Real," *Daily Beast,* October 17, 2008, www.thedailybeast.com/newsweek/2008/10/18/keeping-economics-real.html.

[56] *Huffington Post*, "Eric Bolling Mocks Occupy Wall Street with Tin Foil Hat," *Huffington Post,* October 15, 2011, www.huffingtonpost.com/2011/10/15/eric-bolling-occupy-wall-street_n_1012651.html.

[57] For more analysis of the repeal of the Glass-Steagall Act, four provisions of the Banking Act of 1933, and its role in the current financial crisis, see Paul Krugman, *End This Depression Now!* (New York: W.W. Norton & Co., 2012), Chapters 4, 5, and 7.

[58] "Occupy Wall Street November 12, 2011 Glass-Steagall" uploaded by ReporterWorldNews on November 23, 2011, no longer available, www.youtube.com/watch?v=MwRrw4dNsNY.

[59] John Knefel, "Occupy Defends the Volcker Rule," *Salon,* February 15, 2012, www.salon.com/2012/02/15/occupy_defends_the_volcker_rule/singleton/.

[60] Susan Brooks Thistlethwaite, "Devil in a Pinstripe Suit," On Faith Panelists Blog, *The Washington Post,* March 23, 2009, http://onfaith.washingtonpost.com/onfaith/panelists/susan_brooks_thistlethwaite/2009/03/the_devil_in_a_pinstriped_suit_demonizing_bankers.html.

[61] IMDB. "Wall Street: Money Never Sleeps (2010)," *IMDB*, www.imdb.com/title/tt1027718/.

[62] ThinkProgress War Room, "Mitt Romney Tells the 99% to Stop Being Jealous & Quiet Down," *Think Progress,* January 11, 2012, http://thinkprogress.org/progress-report/mitt-romney-tells-the-99-to-stop-being-jealous-quiet-down/.

[63] Nicholas Confessore, "Campaign Aid Is Now Surging into 8 Figures," *New York Times,* June 13, 2012, www.nytimes.com/2012/06/14/us/politics/sheldon-adelson-sets-new-standard-as-campaign-aid-surges-into-8-figures.html?_r=1&scp=4&sq=June+13+2012&st=nyt; Monica Davey and Jeff Zeleny, "Walker Survives Wisconsin Recall Vote," *New York Times,* June 5, 2012, www.nytimes.com/2012/06/06/us/politics/walker-survives-wisconsin-recall-effort.html?pagewanted=all.

[64] Nick Carey, "In Foreclosures, Occupy Groups See a Unifying Cause," *Reuters,* April 9, 2012, www.reuters.com/article/2012/04/09/us-usa-occupy-foreclosures-idUSBRE8380NO20120409?utm_source=Daily+Digest&utm_campaign=8a796aa519-DD_4_10_124_10_2012&utm_medium=email.

[65] Crossan, *God and Empire,* Ibid., p. 122.

[66] Ibid.

[67] Josephus, *Jewish War,* 2:68.

[68] About.com, search page for Triangle Shirtwaist Factory Fire, www.associatepublisher.com/e/t/tr/triangle_shirtwaist_factory_fire.htm.

[69] Walter Rauschenbusch, *Christianity and the Social Crisis in the 21st Century,* edited by Paul Rauschenbusch (New York: HarperOne, 2007), 40–41.

[70] Ibid., 52–53.

[71] Christopher Thale, "Haymarket and May Day," *Encyclopedia of Chicago,* www.encyclopedia.chicagohistory.org/pages/571.html.

[72] Richard Bradley, "Haymarket Square Riot, *International Encyclopedia of the Social Sciences,* www.encyclopedia.com/topic/Haymarket_Square_riot.aspx.

[73] Ibid.

[74] Stanford University, "Memphis Sanitation Workers Strike (1968)," *Stanford University,* http://mlk-kpp01.stanford.edu/index.php/encyclopedia/encyclopedia/enc_memphis_sanitation_workers_strike_1968/.

[75] The Rev. Dr. Martin Luther King, Jr., "I've Been to the Mountaintop," speech delivered in Memphis, TN, April 3, 1968, www.afscme.org/

union/history/mlk/ive-been-to-the-mountaintop-by-dr-martin-luther-king-jr.

[76] Ibid.

[77] Ibid.

[78] Rev. Dr. Susan Brooks Thistlethwaite, "Progressive Fundamentals: The Dignity of Work,"*Center for American Progress,* February 24, 2009, www.americanprogress.org/issues/2009/02/human_dignity.html.

[79] Susan Brooks Thistlethwaite, "We Need a New Social Gospel: The Moral Imperative of Collective Bargaining," On Faith Panelists Blog, *The Washington Post*, February 23, 2011, http://onfaith.washington post.com/onfaith/panelists/susan_brooks_thistlethwaite/2011/02/we_need_a_new_social_gospel_the_moral_imperative_of_collective_bargaining.html.

[80] *Free Dictionary,* definition of "free market," http://financial-dictionary.thefreedictionary.com/Free-market+capitalism.

[81] Tony Perkins, "My Take: Jesus Was a Free Marketer, Not an Occupier," *CNN,* December 6, 2011, http://religion.blogs.cnn.com/2011/12/06/my-take-jesus-was-a-free-marketer-not-an-occupier/.

[82] Ibid.

[83] Ibid.

[84] Phyllis Tribble, *Texts of Terror: Literary-Feminist Readings of Biblical Narratives* (Fortress Press, 1984).

[85] Richard L. Rohrbaugh, "A Peasant Reading of the Parable of the Talents/Pounds: A Text of Terror?" *BTB* 23 (1993): 32–39.

[86] Ibid., 36.

[87] William R. Herzog II, *Parables as Subversive Speech: Jesus as Pedagogue of the Oppressed* (Louisville, KY: Westminster/John Knox, 1994), 167.

[88] Reuben Guttman, "Fraudsters Lobby to Muzzle Whistleblowers Commentary: Corporations Have Proven They Can't Police Themselves," *Whistleblowerlaws,* October 13, 2011, www.whistleblowerlaws.com/fraudsters-lobby-to-muzzle-whistleblowers-commentary-corporations-have-proven-they-can't-police-themselves/.

[89] I am indebted to John Dominic Crossan's interpretation of this parable from Chapter 5 in his book *The Power of Parable: How Fiction by Jesus Became Fiction About Jesus* (New York: HarperCollins, 2012).

[90] Herzog, 91–95.

[91] National Farmworker Ministry, "Quotes from Cesar Chavez," *National Farmworker Ministry*, http://nfwm.org/2009/04/quotes-from-cesar-chavez/.

[92] Sandra McElwaine, "Hero Grandmother Dolores Huerta Honored with Medal of Freedom," *Daily Beast*, May 18, 2012, www.thedailybeast.com/articles/2012/05/18/hero-grandmother-delores-huerta-honored-with-medal-of-freedom.html.

[93] Randy Shaw, *Beyond the Fields: Cesar Chavez, the UFW, and the Struggle for Justice in the 21st Century* (Berkeley, CA: University of California Press, November 2008).

[94] I would like to thank Dr. Cristian de la Rosa, who makes this point in her dissertation, "Contextual Relationship of Power and Agency: Our Lady of Guadalupe as a Pueblo's Symbolic Resource," May 2012.

[95] Crosby Burns and Jeff Krehely, "Gay and Transgender People Face High Rates of Workplace Discrimination and Harassment," Center for American Progress (June 2, 2011), www.americanprogress.org/issues/2011/06/workplace_discrimination.html.

[96] Seton Hall University School of Law. "Seton Hall Law School Report Shows Immigrant Day Laborers Subjected to Workplace Abuse," *Seton Hall University School of Law*, July 2010, http://law.shu.edu/about/news_events/releases.cfm?id=136966.

[97] Seton Hall University School of Law, "Ironbound Underground Wage Theft & Workplace Violations Among Day Laborers in Newark's East Ward," Seton Hall University School of Law, July 2010, http://law.shu.edu/ProgramsCenters/PublicIntGovServ/CSJ/upload/csj-report-iron bound-underground-july2010.pdf.

[98] Susan Brooks Thistlethwaite, "It's Not 'Class Warfare,' It's Christianity," On Faith Panelists Blog, *The Washington Post*, September 19, 2011, www.washingtonpost.com/blogs/on-faith/post/its-not-class-warfare-its-christianity/2011/09/19/gIQAkoMxfK_blog.html.

[99] Ken Shepherd, "WashPost's 'On Faith' Pounds Pulpit for Tax Hikes on 'The Wealthy,'" *Newsbusters,* September 20, 2011, http://newsbusters.org/blogs/ken-shepherd/2011/09/20/washposts-faith-pounds-pulpit-tax-hikes-rich.

[100] See Sharon H. Ringe, *Jesus, Liberation and the Biblical Jubilee: Images for Ethics and Christology* (Philadelphia, PA: Fortress Press, 1985), Chapter 2.

[101] Ibid., Chapter 3.

[102] Neil Parille, "Ayn Rand, Objectivism, and Religion (Part 1 of 4)," *Rebirth of Reason,* http://rebirthofreason.com/Articles/Parille/Ayn_Rand,_Objectivism,_and_Religion_(Part_1_of_4).shtml.

[103] Jonathan Chait, "War on the Weak," *Daily Beast,* April 10, 2011, www.thedailybeast.com/newsweek/2011/04/10/war-on-the-weak.html.

[104] Ayn Rand, "Excerpt: On Christianity," *Objectivism Resource Center,* www.noblesoul.com/orc/texts/jesus.html.

[105] Jim Wallis, "Woe to You, Legislators!" *Huffington Post,* April 14, 2011, www.huffingtonpost.com/jim-wallis/woe-to-you-legislators_b_849300.html.

[106] Jonathan Easley, "Catholic Bishops Criticize Ryan Budget Cuts to Food Stamps," *The Hill,* April 17, 2012, http://thehill.com/blogs/blog-briefing-room/news/222003-catholic-bishops-criticize-ryan-budget-cuts-to-food-stamps.

[107] Barbara Bradley Hagerty, "Christians Debate: Was Jesus For Small Government?" *National Public Radio,* April 16, 2012, www.npr.org/2012/04/16/150568478/christian-conservatives-poverty-not-government-business.

[108] Paul Krugman, "Death of a Fairy Tale," *New York Times,* April 26, 2012, www.nytimes.com/2012/04/27/opinion/krugman-death-of-a-fairy-tale.html?_r=1.

[109] Alexander Zaitchik, "Protester's New Front," *Salon,* April 23, 2012, www.salon.com/2012/04/23/protesters_furious_new_front/?source=newsletter.

[110] National Public Radio. "Student Loan Debt Exceeds One Trillion Dollars," *National Public Radio,* April 12, 2012, www.npr.org/2012/04/24/151305380/student-loan-debt-exceeds-one-trillion-dollars.

[111] *Forgive Student Loan Debt*, www.forgivestudentloandebt.com/.

[112] *Economist*. "Nope, just debt," *Economist,* October 29, 2011, www.economist.com/node/21534792.

[113] RT. "Debt and Buried: US Students Slaves to Their Loans," *RT,* November 19, 2011, http://rt.com/news/debt-student-loan-gray-737/.

[114] Scott Keyes, "Rep. Virginia Foxx On People With Student Loans: 'I Have Very Little Tolerance' for Them," *Think Progress,* April 13, 2012, http://thinkprogress.org/education/2012/04/13/464154/foxx-tolerance-student-loans/?mobile=nc.

[115] Amy Dean, "Can Occupy Our Homes Move Congress?" *American Prospect,* April 13, 2012, http://prospect.org/article/can-occupy-our-homes-move-congress.

[116] Ajaz Ahmed Khan and Helen Mould, *Islam and Debt*, Islamic Relief Worldwide, April 2008), www.jubileedebtcampaign.org.uk/download.php?id=779.

[117] Steven Hawkins, "Education vs. Incarceration," *American Prospect,* December 6, 2010, http://prospect.org/article/education-vs-incarceration.

[118] Steve Fraser and Joshua Freeman, "Locking Down an American Workforce in the Prison-Corporate Complex," *Common Dreams,* April 19, 2012, www.commondreams.org/view/2012/04/19-4.

[119] Michelle Alexander, *The New Jim Crow: Mass Incarceration in the Age of Colorblindness* (New York: The New Press, 2010); and Michelle Alexander, "The New Jim Crow," *Huffington Post,* February 8, 2010, www.huffingtonpost.com/michelle-alexander/the-new-jim-crow_b_454469.html.

[120] Jim Gerrish, "Magdala, Home of Mary Magdalene," *Church and Israel Forum*, www.churchisraelforum.com/Magdala_home_of_Mary_Magdalene.htm.

[121] Karen L. King, "From the Introduction to: The Gospel of Mary of Magdala: Jesus and the First Woman Apostle," *Gnostic Society Library*, www.gnosis.org/library/GMary-King-Intro.html.

[122] Karen L. King, *The Gospel Of Mary Of Magdala: Jesus and the First Woman Apostle* (Salem, OR: Polebridge Press, 2003).

[123] See, for example, this commentary on the Gospel of Luke from *The Woman's Bible*, www.sacred-texts.com/wmn/wb/wb64.htm.

[124] Leonard Swidler, "Jesus Was a Feminist," *God's Word to Women*, January 1971, www.godswordtowomen.org/feminist.htm.

[125] Letha Scanzoni and Nancy Hardesty, *All We're Meant to Be: A Biblical Approach to Women's Liberation* (Waco, TX: Word Books, 1974).

[126] Susan Brooks Thistlethwaite, "Mary Daly's 'Courage to Sin Big,'" On Faith Panelists Blog, The *Washington Post*, January 5, 2010, http://onfaith.washingtonpost.com/onfaith/panelists/susan_brooks_thistlethwaite/2010/01/the_courage_to_sin_big_the_life_of_mary_daly.html.

[127] Margaret Elizabeth Köstenberger, "Jesus and the Feminists: Case Studies in Feminist Hermeneutics," *Journal of Biblical Manhood and Womanhood*, Spring 2009, http://word4women.wordpress.com/2009/09/19/jesus-and-the-feminists-case-studies-in-feminist-hermeneutics/.

[128] Ibid.

[129] Sharon Ringe, "Luke's Gospel: 'Good News to the Poor' for the Non-Poor," in *The New Testament: Introducing the Way of Discipleship*, edited by Wes Howard-Brook and Sharon H. Ringe (Maryknoll, NY: Orbis Books, 2002), 63–65.

[130] Ibid., 67–68.

[131] Alice Walker, *In Search of Our Mothers' Gardens* (New York: Harcourt, Brace, Jovanovich, 1983), xi.

[132] See Renita Weems, *Just a Sister Away: A Womanist Vision of Women's Relationship in the Bible* (San Diego, CA: LuraMedia, 1988).

[133] Jacqueline Grant, White Women's Christ, Black Women's Jesus: Feminist Christology and Womanist Response (Atlanta, GA: The American Academy of Religion, 1989).

[134] For a much more extensive discussion of womanist perspectives on New Testament biblical interpretation, see Clarice J. Martin, "Womanist Interpretations of the New Testament: The Quest for Wholistic and Inclusive Translation and Interpretation," *Journal of Feminist Studies in Religion*, 6 (2): 41–61.

[135] Katherine Ludwig Jensen, *The Making of the Magdalen: Preaching and Popular Devotion in the Later Middle Ages* (Princeton, NJ: Princeton University Press, 2000), 33, cited in Susan Brooks Thistlethwaite, "Mel Makes a War Movie," *Perspectives on the Passion of the Christ: Religious Thinkers and Writers Explore the Issues Raised by the Controversial Movie* (Miramax Books, 2004), 132.

[136] Ibid.

[137] Susan Brooks Thistlethwaite, "Mel Makes a War Movie," in *Perspectives on the Passion of the Christ: Religious Thinkers and Writers Explore the Issues Raised by the Controversial Movie* (Miramax Books, 2004), 132.

[138] Lorraine Hansberry, *To Be Young, Gifted, and Black* (New York: Penguin Group, 1970).

[139] Adam Peck, "Rush Limbaugh's Advertisers Facing Social Media Firestorm," *Think Progress,* March 2, 2012, http://thinkprogress.org/media/2012/03/02/436852/rush-limbaugh-advertisers/.

[140] "Boycott Rush Limbaugh's Sponsors to SHUT HIM DOWN," Facebook page, www.facebook.com/pages/Boycott-Rush-Limbaughs-Spon sors-to-SHUT-HIM-DOWN/253645602134?sk=wall&filter=12.

[141] Laura Bassett, "Birth Control Access Boosts Women's Wages, Study Finds," *Huffington Post,* March 26, 2012, www.huffingtonpost.com/2012/03/26/birth-control-access-womens-wages_n_1380250.html?ref=politics&ir=Politics.

[142] Planned Parenthood, "Survey: Nearly Three in Four Voters in America Support Fully Covering Prescription Birth Control," *Planned Parenthood,* July 2010, www.plannedparenthood.org/about-us/newsroom/press-releases/survey-nearly-three-four-voters-america-support-fully-covering-prescription-birth-control-33863.htm.

[143] Bryce Covert, "The Fast Pace of Change for Women Workers Can't Distract From the Work Left to Do," *Nation,* March 26, 2012,

www.thenation.com/blog/167045/fast-pace-change-women-workers-cant-distract-work-left-do?utm_source=Daily+Digest&utm_campaign=997cfae6ba-DD_3_27_123_27_2012&utm_medium=email.

[144] Tamura A. Lomax, "Occupy Rape Culture," *Feminist Wire,* November 5, 2011, http://thefeministwire.com/2011/11/occupy-rape-culture/.

[145] Sarah Seltzer, "Where Are the Women at Occupy Wall Street? Everywhere—and They're Not Going Away," *Nation,* October 26, 2011, www.thenation.com/article/164197/where-are-women-occupy-wall-street-everywhere-and-theyre-not-going-away.

[146] Rita Nakashima Brock and Susan Brooks Thistlethwaite, *Casting Stones: Prostitution in Asia and the United States* (Minneapolis, MN: Fortress Press, 1996).

[147] Rita Nakashima Brock, "The Obama Legacy at Occupy Oakland," *Huffington Post,* October 27, 2011, www.huffingtonpost.com/rita-nakashima-brock-ph-d/occupy-oakland-obama_b_1035429.html.

[148] Rita Nakashima Brock and Rebecca Parker, *Saving Paradise: How Christianity Traded Love of this World for Crucifixion and Empire,* http://savingparadise.net/reviews/.

[149] Andrew Cohen, "The Torture Memos, Ten Years Later," *The Atlantic* (Feb. 6, 2012), www.theatlantic.com/national/archive/2012/02/the-torture-memos-10-years-later/252439/.

[150] Jane Mayer, *The Dark Side: The Inside Story of How the War on Terror Turned into a War on American Ideals* (New York: Doubleday, 2008), 245.

[151] Elaine Scarry, *The Body in Pain: The Making and Unmaking of the World* (New York: Oxford University Press, 1985), Chapter 1.

[152] Ibid.

[153] Mayer, p. 256.

[154] Bill Moyers and Michael Winship, "Bill Moyers: When Will Americans Face the Horrific Truth? We're a Nation of Torturers," *AlterNet,* May 25, 2012, www.alternet.org/world/155601/bill_moyers:_when_will_americans_face_the_horrific_truth_we're_a_nation_of_torturers?page=entire.

155 Tom Head, "The Posse Comitatus Act of 1878," *About.com Civil Liberties*, http://civilliberty.about.com/od/waronterror/a/posse_act.htm.

156 Radley Balko, "A Decade After 9/11, Police Departments Are Increasingly Militarized," *Huffington Post*, September 11, 2011, www.huffingtonpost.com/2011/09/12/police-militarization-9-11-september-11_n_955508.html.

157 Ibid.

158 Al Baker, "When the Police Go Military," *New York Times*, December 3, 2011, www.nytimes.com/2011/12/04/sunday-review/have-american-police-become-militarized.html?pagewanted=all.

159 Ibid.

160 PressTV, "EU Austerity Policies Can Ignite Uncontrolled Unrest: Analyst," *PressTV*, May 4, 2012, www.presstv.ir/detail/239505.html.

161 Victor Gold, Thomas Hoyt Jr., Sharon Ringe, Susan Thistlethwaite, Burton Throckmorton, and Barbara Withers, *New Testament and Psalms: An Inclusive Version* (New York and Oxford: Oxford University Press, 1995).

162 Doug Mataconis, "The Death Of Occupy Wall Street? It Sure Seems Like It," *Outside the Beltway*, May 17, 2012, www.outsidethebeltway.com/the-death-of-occupy-wall-street-it-sure-seems-like-it/.

163 Pew Forum on Religion and Public Life "Religion Among the Millennials," *Pew Forum on Religion and Public Life*, February 17, 2010, www.pewforum.org/Age/Religion-Among-the-Millennials.aspx.

164 MillennialsThinkTank,"Hypocritical and Judgemental? Church Maybe, Jesus Never," *millenialsthinktank*, February 9, 2012, http://millennialsthinktank.com/2012/02/09/hypocritical-judgemental-church-maybe-jesus-never/.

165 "Why I Hate Religion, But Love Jesus," uploaded January 10, 2012, no longer available, www.youtube.com/watch?v=1IAhDGYlpqY.

166 Elizabeth Tenety, "'Why I Hate Religion, But Love Jesus' goes viral," *Washington Post*, January 18, 2012, www.washingtonpost.com/blogs/under-god/post/why-i-hate-religion-but-love-jesus-goes-viral/2012/01/18/gIQARzXp8P_blog.html.

[167] J. Deotis Roberts, *Bonhoeffer and King: Speaking Truth to Power* (Louisville, KY: Westminster John Knox Press, 2005), 46–47.

[168] Dietrich Bonhoeffer, *The Cost of Discipleship* (New York: Simon and Schuster, Inc., 1995), originally published 1937.

[169] Pew Research Center, "41%—Jesus Christ's Return to Earth," *Pew Research Center,* April 21–26, 2010, http://pewresearch.org/databank/dailynumber/?NumberID=1043.

[170] Joseph E. Stiglitz and Linda J. Bilmes, "The $3 Trillion War," *Vanity Fair,* April 2008, www.vanityfair.com/politics/features/2008/04/stiglitz200804.

[171] Richard Kogan and Paul N. Van de Water, "Romney Budget Proposals Would Require Massive Cuts in Medicare, Medicaid, and Other Programs," *Center on Budget and Policy Priorities,* May 21, 2012, www.cbpp.org/cms/index.cfm?fa=view&id=3658.

[172] Michelle A. Vu, "Fla. Megachurch Pastor Joel Hunter: Impossible for Church to Feed Poor in Place of Gov't," *Christian Post,* April 11, 2012, www.christianpost.com/news/fla-megachurch-pastor-joel-hunter-impossible-for-church-to-feed-poor-in-place-of-govt-73072/.

[173] David Gushee, ed., *A New Evangelical Manifesto: A Kingdom Vision for the Common Good,* Chalice Press, August, 2012. www.chalicepress.com/A-New-Evangelical-Manifesto-P1029.aspx.

[174] Ibid.

[175] www.catholicsinalliance.org/.

[176] www.networklobby.org/.

[177] Harlan Beckley, "Reflections on the Life of Monsignor John A. Ryan" in *Religion and Public Life: The Legacy of Monsignor John A. Ryan*, ed. Robert G. Kennedy, Mary Christine Athans, Bernard V. Brady, William C. McDonough, and Michael J. Naughton (Lanham: University Press of America, 2001), 7, *Laborem Exercens,* www.vatican.va/holy_father/john_paul_ii/encyclicals/documents/hf_jp-ii_enc_14091981_laborem-exercens_en.html; The National Council of Catholic Bishops, *The Challenge of Peace: God's Promise and Our Response*, http://old.usccb.org/sdwp/international/TheChallengeofPeace.pdf.

[178] *Goodreads,* Anne Lamott quotes page, www.goodreads.com/author/quotes/71130.Anne_Lamott.

[179] Michelle Boorstein, "American Nuns Stunned by Vatican Accusation of 'Radical Feminism,' Crackdown," *Washington Post,* April 20, 2012, www.washingtonpost.com/local/american-nuns-stunned-by-vatican-accusation-of-radical-feminism-crackdown/2012/04/20/gIQAi4gkWT_story.html.

[180] John Gehring, "A Brave Catholic Pastor Defends Nuns, Blasts Vatican Crackdown," *Faith in Public Life,* May 30, 2012, www.faithinpubliclife.org/blog/a-brave-catholic-pastor-defends-nuns-blasts-vatican-crackdown/.

[181] Nuns on the Bus: Nuns Drive for Faith, Family, and Fairness, http://nunsonthebus.com/.

[182] NETWORK, A National Catholic Social Justice Lobby, www.networklobby.org/.

[183] Laurie Goodstein, "Nuns, Rebuked by Rome, Plan Road Trip to Spotlight Social Issues," *New York Times,* June 12, 2012, www.nytimes.com/2012/06/06/us/us-nuns-bus-tour-to-spotlight-social-issues.html.

[184] Colin Moynihan, "Trespassing Case Adds Strain to Trinity Church's Ties with Occupy Protesters," *New York Times,* June 10, 2012, www.nytimes.com/2012/06/11/nyregion/trespassing-case-adds-strain-to-churchs-ties-with-occupy-protesters.html.

[185] Sharon Sheridan, "Trinity Wall Street: Episcopal Clergy Convicted After 'Occupy' Demonstration on Church Property," *Huffington Post,* June 19, 2012, www.huffingtonpost.com/2012/06/19/trinity-wall-street-occupy_n_1610651.html.

[186] Ibid.

[187] Jennifer Butler, "The Golden Calf and Occupy Wall Street," *Huffington Post,* October 13, 2011, www.huffingtonpost.com/rev-jennifer-butler/golden-calf-occupy-wall-street_b_1009455.html.

[188] Donna Schaper, "Occupy Wall Street, The Golden Calf and the New Idolatry," *Huffington Post,* November 11, 2011, www.huffing

tonpost.com/donna-schaper/occupy-wall-street-the-go_b_1004946.html#s402665&title=Faith_Occupies_Wall.

[189] Peter Laarman, personal communication, June 5, 2012.

[190] Ibid.

[191] James Forbes, "The Next Great Awakening," *Tikkun*, September/October 2010, www.tikkun.org/article.php/sept2010forbes.

[192] Diana Butler Bass, *Christianity After Religion: The End of Church and the Birth of a New Spiritual Awakening* (San Francisco: HarperOne, 2012), 223.

[193] Quest For Meaning, www.livestream.com/questformeaning/.

[194] Susan Brooks Thistlethwaite, *Dreaming of Eden: American Religion and Politics in a Wired World* (New York: Palgrave/Macmillan, 2010).